C

Food Lovers' Guide

A Compendium of Words, Facts, Folklore, Recipes & History

A.H. Jackson

Lone Pine Publishing
10145 – 81 Avenue
Edmonton, AB T6E 1W9
Canada

Website: www.lonepinepublishing.com

Library and Archives Canada Cataloguing in Publication

Jackson, A.H., 1944-
            Canadian food lovers' guide : a compendium of
words, facts, folklore, recipes and history / A.H. Jackson.

Includes bibliographical references.
ISBN 978-1-55105-638-8

            1. Food--Miscellanea. 2. Food habits--Canada. 3. Cookery--Canada. I. Title.

TX360.C3J33 2010   641.300971   C2010-901785-4

Editorial Director: Nancy Foulds
Project Editor: Sheila Quinlan
Production Manager: Gene Longson
Layout and Production: Lisa Morley
Production Support: Rob Tao
Cover Design: Gerry Dotto
Cover Images: roast turkey © 2006 Seattle Support Group; fish © Jupiterimages; tomatoes ©
www.imagesource.com; cheese © Zedcor Wholly Owned; bread loaf © 2006 DigitalPixs;
asparagus © Hemera Technologies; parsley © Hemera Technologies; grapes © Hemera
Technologies; poutine © Merle Prosofsky MPA; all other photos © Photos.com.

Photos: All-America Selections 214; Jen Fafard 78, 94; Derek Fell 37, 203; Olga
Langerova 58; Photos.com 33, 52, 100, 140, 160; Laura Peters 220, 247; Merle Prosofsky
47, 59, 72, 75, 88, 124, 130, 152, 153, 185, 189, 200, 204, 206, 211, 213, 224, 234, 244,
253, 267; Nanette Samol 41, 53, 62, 84, 93, 104, 117, 143, 197, 201, 228.

Illustrations: Frank Burman 44, 56a&b, 60, 115, 130, 136, 157, 175, 181, 183, 186, 190,
198, 228a&b, 249b, 264; Gary Ross 49, 55, 63, 75, 77, 108, 114, 180, 222, 223, 238; Ian
Sheldon 33, 41, 50, 54, 71, 73, 87, 98, 105, 113, 118, 120, 126, 138, 139, 158, 168, 182,
185, 192, 225, 229, 236a&b, 245, 249a, 259, 262, 266, 268.

We acknowledge the financial support of the Government of Canada through the Book
Publishing Industry Development Program (BPIDP) for our publishing activities.

PC: 1

Table of Contents

Introduction

This book is for those Canadians made uncomfortable by the ubiquitous end game offerings on all Chinese restaurant menus—the Canadian food section: cheeseburgers, frits and fried chicken. There is more, you know there has to be, but somehow you cannot put a finger on what else besides poutine, butter tarts and maple-flavoured doughnuts. You are not alone, as almost every Canadian is afflicted with a kind of nationalistic dementia generated by successive tidal waves of 20th-century convenience foods. A cuisine of centuries has been suborned by frozen entrées and branded quickie foods to a point that dinner tables have become redundant in most Canadian households.

In an 1833 letter to home, a year after immigrating to Canada, author, amateur botanist and pioneer advocate Catharine Parr Traill inventoried the skills required of pioneer women: they must know how to tap maple trees to make sugar; they must know how to make vinegar, candles, soap and bread; they must know how to produce hop rising, to salt meat and fish, to spin, dye and knit yarn; they must make clothes, manage chickens, rear and keep cattle and know how to milk cows and churn butter.

In 1836, Catharine Parr Traill's famous account of her first years in Canada was published in Britain, where it became a bestseller. Her follow up book, *The Female Emigrant's Guide and Hints on Canadian Housekeeping*, published in 1854, quickly became the emigrant's bible. Among her many helpful tips to prospective settlers is one that became a supreme benefit to both pioneer families and the whole of Canada: bring seeds. The early French settlers brought apples, peas and onions; Scotsmen brought oatmeal and turnips; the English brought pears, peaches, cherries and rhubarb; and the Irish brought their potatoes.

Unlike the vast majority of American settlers, most Canadian pioneers arrived with a plan and prepared for hardships. They had studied maps, read books, knew their destination, the climate and what difficulties lay in store. While the U.S. invited the poor and downtrodden, Britain insisted land grant immigrants to Canada be skilled and financially secure; tradesmen went to the towns and villages, skilled farmers to the immediate countryside and Highland Scots and Irish to the hinterlands. Britain recruited millers to operate "crown mills," assisted settlers in procuring livestock and supplied law and order. The colonization of Canada progressed westward in an orderly fashion, unlike in the U.S., where expansion always outran the law, creating wild frontiers. In Canada, settlers got right to work; men cleared land, built cabins and planted crops, while the women supplied brainpower and direction: what to plant first, where to plant it, how to use and sell the surplus and what to eat in the meantime.

One can almost visualize the pioneer wife, one arm akimbo, the other outstretched and shaking a finger at her husband. "Samuel," she says, "you make that fireplace hearth much larger. I will not be on hands and knees whilst I cook thy dinner." She would get her larger hearth, because in the New World, women ruled. Women decided where to build, what to build and how big. They laid out and planted vegetable gardens, had charge of finances, clothed and fed their family and got them all to church on time. If there were no churches, they arranged a community raising and got them built. Women were the nucleus, the driving force that populated this great nation, and when things got tough, they were always there to point out that better days were just ahead.

For early settlers who depended on fresh produce, the months of April and May were the hardest; root cellars were exhausted, cows were off their milking, and foraging in the wild took on new meaning: survival. Forests were a boon to early Canadians, who also enjoyed another benefit not usually available to pioneers in the U.S.: a watery lifeline, the St. Lawrence River and the Great Lakes. Early settlements were never far from this river and lake system that allowed settlers access to the sea and the far-off market of Great Britain. Canada had vast quantities of fish and timber for sale or trade, and the ships that arrived to buy and transport those commodities to France, Britain and her colonies never arrived empty. They carried livestock from France, molasses, citrus, dried fruits and salt from the Caribbean and spices, tobacco, tea and coffee from the east, via Britain. General stores at the very fringes of civilization rarely stocked refined sugar or flour, but molasses, lemons, apples, oranges, tea, spices and coconut might be there by the barrel full. The availability of food items rare in the U.S. helped to shape Canadian cuisine, but similarities existed in the use of wild game and natural forest products, and, of course, there were ties that bound them to the home country.

Canada belonged to Britain until Confederation in 1867, and while settlement in the U.S. was helter-skelter, Canada enjoyed a government-supervised colonization. Settlers had to prove their worth before receiving property deeds, British law was always close at hand and relations with First Nations seldom derailed as they did south of the border. Friendly relations meant closer contact with native peoples, and from them, early settlers received much-needed advice on living in the wilds. The cuisine of First Nations saw a welcome adoption by our early settlers, and both their recipes and preparation techniques feature predominantly in the evolution of the great Canadian food experience. Helping thy neighbour was an important part of pioneer life, both north and south of the border; however, prairie farms in Canada tended to be smaller and closer together than in the U.S., which allowed for a greater degree of neighbourly assistance when needed.

Canadian pioneers often brought belongings from the home country, while in the U.S. they generally arrived penniless, with only the clothes on their backs. To have books, lamps to read by, seeds to plant, pots, pans, a fireplace crane and spices to cook with helped to assure pioneer families that better days were around the corner. Acquiring a cow, pigs and chickens were the first of those better days for pioneer families, and procuring these animals changed lives. Milk, butter, pork, chicken and fresh eggs were the nightly dreams of every new settler until the big day arrived. Imagine the excitement the first pail of milk created, or the screams of delight over that first egg. Pioneering in Canada had its moments, and one of the biggest, especially for the pioneer wife, had to be the finished kitchen, with a window, from where she could watch her future unfold and keep an eye on her garden and cooling pies.

Early settlers ate a lot of pies: game pies, fruit pies, chicken pies, wild berry pies, pork pies, custard pies, turnip and potato pies and, now and then, beef pies. A cow for milk and butter, a field of wheat and a barrel of salt meant short-crust pie pastry, and a way to transform fruit, berries and meats into portable culinary delights that stayed fresh in cool root cellars for weeks. The pie featured predominantly in our historical food experience and, with or without crusts, remains a bulwark of modern-day Canadian cuisine: one-pot meals, casseroles, braised meats and even microwave convenience foods evolved from the pie, a culinary masterpiece with a long history.

History has moulded our national character and provided Canadians with decent values. We cherish law and order, we do not riot in the streets, we respect our neighbours and we tolerate different political and religious beliefs. We are nice people of many origins united in one goal: to make Canada the best it can be in everything. We are doing a good job, because Canada is prime living space on the planet and one of the world's great food producers. We feed so many, yet so few of us know anything about our great Canadian food experience, or how it evolved from backwoods survival rations to become the national cuisine. For your erudition, allow me to present our national cuisine timeline.

Canadian Cuisine Milestones

1497

Giovanni Caboto, *aka* John Cabot, sails off from Bristol, England, to find a short trade route to the Orient. Three months later, he returns to report finding a whole New World of tall trees and waters so thick with fish they could be hauled aboard in buckets. In 15th-century England, fish was a magic word, and Cabot's stories earned him a second five-ship voyage in 1497. It was a fateful one, because he failed to survive, but several of his ships returned to corroborate his fishy tales, and not long after whole fleets from France, Spain and England were braving the western sea and searching out the fish that could be caught in buckets…cod.

1534

Jacques Cartier encounters the Mi'kmaq, and some trade ensues, an occasion that will eventually set off a mad rush for furs. He also sails into the Gulf of St. Lawrence to Chaleur Bay, where he encounters a group of Iroquois come to hunt seals. While only the encounter is noted in Cartier's log, he and his

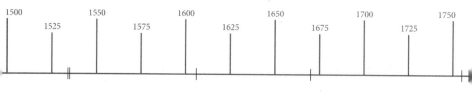

crew must have been treated to a dinner: seal, cod and sturgeon, maple sugar–glazed moose loin, corn soup and cakes, all washed down with spruce beer. Cartier repays that hospitality by kidnapping two of the chief's sons and taking them back to France as souvenirs. They're smart kids, because on the way they hatch a plan that guarantees their return; they simply play on the Frenchmen's greed and tell them about all the gold in a place called "the Kingdom of the Saguenay."

1535

Cartier is back with the kids looking for riches, and while he finds none, his discovery of another gold, the Iroquois cornfields, will eventually reap far more benefit to Europe than the real thing. This time, Cartier kidnaps the Iroquois headman, Chief Donnacona, who succeeds in making his kids' fabricated story of Saguenay gold even more convincing. In 1541, Cartier returns to New France, but without Chief Donnacona, who has died in France. This news puts off the Iroquois, who quickly lay siege to Cartier's settlement. Cartier may have been run off, but he doesn't care because he has found gold and diamonds. He returns to France triumphant, but is forced into retirement when his riches turn out to be worthless quartz and iron pyrites: fool's gold. The end of Cartier's explorations marked the beginning of Europe's run for the fish, and by 1580, over 10,000 Europeans were making the annual journey across the pond to fish for cod. The New World had become a beehive of exploitation, and new foods were discovered: strawberries, corn, potatoes, peanuts, chocolate, avocados, tomatoes, chili peppers, pineapples—and the list goes on and on.

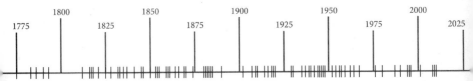

1606

Cartographer and explorer Samuel de Champlain, having barely survived a disastrous first winter on an island in the St. Lawrence, establishes a new settlement on the mainland, calling it Port Royal. Applying lessons learned during the previous hard winter, he institutes an eating club, *L'Ordre de Bon Temps*, the Order of Good Cheer, and orders that 15 of the most prominent members of his all-male settlement take turns hosting special meals. It was a good idea; it caused a culinary competition within the whole group, resulting in joyous camaraderie, better nutrition and an easier wait for spring. Disbanded in the spring of 1607, the Order of Good Cheer has become legend, especially in Quebec, where the feasts of *Bon Temp* are recreated every winter.

1670

King Charles II grants the lands of the Hudson Bay watershed to "the Governor and Company of Adventurers Trading into Hudson's Bay," and the great rush to riches is off and running. Calling itself the Hudson's Bay Company, the group sent out capable managers they called factors to establish fur trading posts called factories and kept them well supplied with trade goods and food. To keep the factors happy and reward the voyageurs who ferried furs to Montreal and returned with supplies, the HBC made sure every factory was well stocked with butter, tea, biscuits, coffee, cane sugar, salt beef and all the goodies from home, a nice tradition that would in later years provide pioneer families with a bit of the home country.

1755

The deportation of French-speaking Acadians from Nova Scotia, New Brunswick and New England begins. Many are transported to France, but most are dispersed to southern areas of North America, with thousands finding their way to Louisiana, where they become known as Cajuns. Years later, almost half the

Acadians return to Canada, bringing not only their old Acadian cuisine but also their new Cajun style of cooking.

1759

The washerwomen of Quebec City's Lower Town inadvertently supply British troops a way to surprise and defeat the French garrison at Quebec City. Having observed the women washing clothes in the river, the British simply waited for nightfall and proceeded single file up the path the women used to descend and ascend the cliff with their washing. With the British in complete control of Canada, the French/Indian threat to her 13 southern colonies disappeared, enabling those colonies to concentrate on freeing themselves from British control. Immigration to Canada from the Thirteen Colonies and Britain increases; ships loaded with settlers arrive almost daily, and the evolving Canadian food experience switches from a pork, fish, wine and sauce-based cuisine to one built upon mutton, beef, peas and beer. English-style taverns become popular, the beer flows and roast beef with mushy peas almost decimates the Canadian food experience.

1775

The American Revolution begins, and the action creates a political and military front, or border, with Canada where none had previously existed. Political and military posturing uproots families on both sides, while both overseas and St. Lawrence shipping slows to a trickle. Staples such as salt, molasses, spices, citrus, tea and coffee become unavailable. The few general stores serving pioneer settlements close up, and families must rely on foraged foods and ingenuity to survive.

1783

United Empire Loyalists fleeing the American Revolution arrive in all parts of Upper Canada and the Maritimes. They bring both their cuisine and their slaves, with each having an impact on the evolution of Canadian cuisine—roast duck laced with cayenne pepper is a culinary revelation for Canadian settlers.

1786

John Molson buys a small brewery in Montreal and begins creating a financial, nation-expanding empire that will include banks, lumber, steamships, a railway and larger breweries. Called the nation's greatest entrepreneur, John Molson and his business endeavours created a demand for timber and grains, while his banks brought needed capital to small towns and villages. In 1825, he built the British American Hotel in downtown Montreal; modelled after the Palais Royal in Paris and managed by an Italian hosteler, Molson's hotel and dining room, the finest in North America, became a benchmark for future great Canadian hotels.

1790

A salt boiling operation is established at Twelve Mile Creek (now St. Catharines, Ontario) by William Merritt, an immigrant from Liverpool, England, a city with a long history of salt production. The British government in Upper Canada discontinues the practice of supplying each settler family with a barrel of imported salt.

1793

Slavery, called indentured servitude, is abolished in what is now Ontario; wealthy landowners depending on indentured workers and kitchen help either downsize, leave the province for the U.S. or go to Quebec, where the practice of indentured servitude continues until 1833.

1812

The U.S. declares war on Britain, and conflict breaks out along the Canada–U.S. border. Shipping on the St. Lawrence slows to a trickle, and men leave their farms and families to fight. U.S. forces burn York (Toronto) and capture the British fleet on Lake

Erie. Canadian militia, British regulars and First Nations warriors capture Detroit and burn the American cities of Washington and Buffalo. Upper Canada general stores close for lack of merchandise, and hard-pressed pioneer families look to the forests for survival.

1816

The infamous "year without summer" caused by an 1815 volcanic eruption in Sumatra forces many settlers to abandon farms in what is now eastern Canada and move westward into the central regions.

1817

The side-wheel steamship *Frontenac*, built in Bath, near Kingston, begins plying the waters of Lake Ontario. She ferries in supplies to settlers and takes out potash, furs and timber.

1818

Canada's first sugar refinery opens in Halifax but is of little benefit to settlers down the line. They make do with homemade maple sugar, an arduous, time-consuming endeavour, or they purchase barrels of molasses or expensive, poor-quality muscovado, sometimes called Barbados sugar, from suppliers in Montreal. *Muscovado* means "unrefined" in Spanish, and it arrived at the port of Montreal in molasses-dripping kegs with their dirty brown contents half fermented.

1821

The Hudson's Bay Company and its archrival the North West Company merge, giving HBC a continent-wide reach.

1825

Unescorted ladies are allowed access to John Molson's new Montreal hotel, the British American, something unheard of in Europe and a custom continued in all newly built Canadian hotels.

1828

The Welland Canal opens, but with a depth of only 4 feet, it proves unsatisfactory; reconstruction begins immediately.

1832

The opening of the Rideau Canal enables shipping from Halifax to Welland, in what is now Ontario, and beyond via the Welland Canal.

1833

The Welland Canal reopens with a depth of 8 feet. It is now able to handle vessels coming all the way from Halifax via the Rideau Canal. For residents of Canada West, life improves considerably; more general stores open, and goods sold become more varied and less expensive. Millers get larger grinding stones and equipment to harness waterpower, Great Lakes fishermen receive salt, and lumbermen have a way to ship their products to the east coast and beyond.

1835

Justus von Liebig, a German chemist and inventor of chloroform, nitrogen fertilizer and the meat extract OXO, experiments with various combinations of powdered acids and sodium bicarbonate (baking soda) and invents what every housewife has been waiting for: baking powder. Milk no longer needs clabbering (souring, acidification) to provide a rising for baked goods and breads, and cakes and cookies no longer taste of ammonia through the use of ammonium bicarbonate, the precursor to baking powder.

However, housewives would continue to wait until 1843, when English chemist Alfred Bird produces a workable baking powder by combining sodium bicarbonate (baking soda) with cream of tartar and cornstarch. That was fine and dandy for European bakers, but housewives in North America were still clabbering dough and waiting for 1855, when Eben Norton Horsford, of Providence, Rhode Island, discovered that calcium phosphate and baking soda work to raise bread and began to market Rumford Baking Powder in bulk. In 1866, two brothers, Joseph and Cornelius Hoagland, along with a young marketing genius named William Ziegler, gave both American and Canadian housewives a convenient, branded product they called Royal Baking Powder. A year later, two New Englanders, John Dwight and James Church, launched their Cow Brand, a baking powder that became immensely popular in Canada. In 1885, a German pharmacist, Dr. Oetker, discovered that aluminium sulphate will cause baked goods to rise in a hot oven. Three years later, in 1888, baking powder salesman William Monroe Wright (a cousin of Wilbur and Orville Wright) had an idea to combine sodium aluminium phosphate and cream of tartar. This double-action baking powder raises baked goods before and during the baking. His company, the Calumet Baking Powder Company, became the world's largest manufacturer of baking powder. Double action is a good idea, and the year before Wright's Calumet brand hits the market, the E.W. Gillette Company of Chicago launches its Magic brand, another double-action baking powder, beating Calumet to the Canadian market. Both Cow Brand and Magic baking powders ruled ovens from Ontario to the eastern seaboard, while the Royal brand held sway in western Canada, with all brands manufactured in Canada after the turn of the century.

1837

Armed insurrection in both Upper and Lower Canada (the Rebellion) is crushed, with most of the instigators, including leaders William Lyon Mackenzie and Louis-Joseph Papineau, escaping to the U.S. Armed incursions by American irregular forces keeps tensions high along the border and hampers ship traffic on the St. Lawrence, forcing settlers to rely on the forests for survival—again.

1841

An Englishman named Orlando Jones gets the idea to grind hominy (the endosperm of corn) into starch in an alkaline bath. Jones managed to secure both British and American patents on his brainwave, but Canadian mills paid them no heed and quickly installed corn boilers, alkaline baths and reset their grinding stones to very fine. In no time at all, cheap cornstarch had replaced expensive arrowroot and tapioca starch in every Canadian kitchen. More pies and puddings put smiles on the faces of overworked farmers and settlers, prompting the government in Ottawa to ignore Orlando Jones' demands for patent protection.

1846

Waves of Irish immigrants arrive in Canada to escape the potato famine, bringing with them cholera and typhus, which spreads to both urban and rural areas of Canada and kills almost 20 percent of the population. Canadians stick to their farms and homes, and kitchens take on a new importance.

1847

A stamping machine to mass produce tin cans is patented by American inventor Henry Evens, and tin cans slowly become available countrywide. Canning bees are popular, with area families sharing in the cost of a canning machine. Local women spend days preparing food and filling, boiling and cranking the machine, while their men haul cans and install shelves in root cellars. A taste of summer enjoyed in the dead of winter considerably improves the lives of settlers, prompting the creation of new and distinctly Canadian recipes.

1850

Specifically designed cooking stoves begin to appear, completely changing the culinary practices of Canadian cooks. Up to this date, wood- or coal-fired stoves were designed solely for heating, with housewives still labouring in the kitchen hearth over one-pot or roasted meals. In 1854, Toronto resident Ruth Adams received the first patent granted by the British government to a Canadian woman for what she called the reverse cooking stove. More efficient than a regular stove, it could heat, bake, boil and fry, but her design never saw manufacturing, probably owing to cost of production. The average Canadian family had little money to spend, and while the kitchen stove quickly gained acceptance, most were procured from local iron foundries and were cheap iron boxes with doors. But even so crude a device would cause users to think they had died and gone to heaven; no more red faces from cooking in an open hearth, no more pie and bread with soggy centres, no more hauling tons of wood and no more chimney fires, and the stoves had room for multiple cooking pots—what a relief. However, it would be another 20 years before factory-manufactured cooking stoves became widely available. Probably the best was the Findlay Stove, made at the Findlay Foundry, Carlton Place. This Canadian success story continues to this day—Findlay Stove is still in the business of manufacturing wood-burning ovens and stoves, along with many modern appliances.

1853

The Grand Trunk Railway is created through the amalgamation of six railways, completing a line from the east coast to Toronto. That same year, the Great Western Railway completes a track from Niagara Falls to Windsor, with a spur to Toronto. It is now possible to travel and ship goods from Halifax to Windsor. It is a huge break for settlers in Canada West (Ontario), who now have access to food items as diverse as fresh oysters, lobsters, salt, sugar, woollen goods and heavy machinery.

1854

John Redpath, a construction contractor for the Rideau Canal, opens a sugar refinery in Montreal, and life is suddenly a whole lot sweeter for Canada's settlers.

1855

Canned meats, soups and pork and beans become available in urban food and rural general stores.

1859

The government of the Province of Canada creates Thanksgiving Day, a Canadian original, as the U.S. did not institute the holiday until the end of the Civil War.

1860

Glass canning jars become available to settlers in eastern Canada. Called Mason jars, after the inventor John L. Mason, the screw-top containers revolutionize home canning and turn root cellars into glittering depositories of summer delights. Not until the completion of the railway in 1885 will the canning jars become widely available in western Canada.

1861

William Davies opens a meat-packing plant in Toronto, an operation that will eventually become the mighty Canada Packers Limited.

1864

French aristocrat Justin de Courtenay cultivates European grapes on the western shore of Lake Ontario and forms a company called Vine Growers Association. At the 1867 Paris Exposition, his Gamay grape wine wins a prize, a feat not repeated by a Canadian winery for another century.

1866

Samuel Platt discovers salt while drilling for oil in Goderich, Ontario. Platt starts a company to process brine from his drill site, and according to judges at the 1867 Paris Exposition, produces the world's finest salt. Salt is no longer an expensive import for settlers and becomes widely available. Cheaper salt prompts the formation of Great Lakes fisheries, along with many meat and fowl preserving companies, which is a boon to pioneer families headed west.

1869

The Hudson's Bay Company signs a "deed of surrender" with the Canadian government giving up all claims of ownership to that vast area of North America called Rupert's Land. The company's focus changes from furs to goods, and trading posts (called factories) stock more varied merchandise.

1870

The first salmon cannery is established at Annieville, British Columbia. Cans containing 1 pound of fish are hand packed and soldered, and the first year's production is around 300 cases. Ten years later, three canneries are shipping cases across the country and to Europe, and production climbs to 100,000 cases. By the year 1900, over 90 canneries are in operation, shipping out over 2 million cases of a product that changes the eating habits of Canadians. Cheap and readily available, the 1-pound tins of BC salmon spawn many enduring recipes.

1874

Toronto medical student Henry Woodward invents the electric light bulb and illuminates his mother's kitchen. The next year he sells his patent to American inventor Thomas Edison and buys his mother a Findlay stove for her brand-new kitchen.

1880

Red Fife wheat seed, an accidental discovery by Ontario farmer David Fife, is made available to all prairie farmers. Grain storage elevators holding around 35,000 bushels are constructed 15 kilometres apart beside rail lines, causing towns and villages to spring up almost overnight.

1881

La Compagnie de Sucre de Betterave de Quebec begins refining sugar from beets in Farnam, Quebec. Two decades later, Ontario has four large sugar beet refineries, and within a short time, both Alberta and Manitoba have refineries. Today, only Quebec, Manitoba and Alberta have factories processing sugar beets, a shrinking industry owing to competition from American high-fructose corn-syrup producers.

1882

Ottawa engineer and businessman Thomas Ahearn invents the electric cooking range for the kitchen of Ottawa's Windsor Hotel. That same year, he invents and patents an electric heater, water heater and flat iron. Six years later, Ahearn's Ottawa Electric Company illuminates the entire city, and two years after that, he has electric streetcars running the length of the city. However, many years would pass before the average Canadian housewife would benefit from his electric range or other inventions, as generating electricity and stringing power lines became a slow process. Natural gas is cheap, easier to produce and pipe and beat electricity into Canadian kitchens by decades.

1883

Successive crop failures put the future of prairie farming in doubt. Just in time, old bones emerge from the parched landscape to save farmers from rack and ruin. By 1890, bison bones become the Prairies' largest export. Shipped by rail car to eastern cities, the bones were converted to phosphate fertilizer and the carbon used to refine sugar. During the decade from 1883 to 1893, the gathered-up bones of over 1 million bison were loaded onto rail cars and shipped east for processing. The greatest crime perpetrated on wildlife was the indiscriminate slaughter of millions of plains buffalo, but the bones saved an agricultural endeavour slated to become one of the world's great breadbaskets.

1884

The T. Eaton Company begins filling mail orders for goods and provisions with shipping by rail to the nearest depot. Canadian Pacific Railway tracks had reached Calgary by then, and Eaton's establishes a special department to handle orders and shipments to western settlers. Eaton's issues a catalogue of goods available and gives western farmers a taste of the good life. Orders pour into Eaton's for all manner of dry and canned goods. The lives of western farm wives improves considerably when Eaton's begins shipping stoves.

1885

Our transcontinental railway is complete and the future of Canada's grain industry assured. Prairie housewives now have access to necessities that make their lives endurable. New settlers arrive accompanied by their worldly possessions, while at the same time, cook stove, piano and cream separator salesmen fan out across the Prairies.

1890

Emile Paturel opens a lobster-canning factory at Shediac, New Brunswick, and although he goes broke three times, he eventually manages to turn the bottom-crawling crustacean into a culinary treat he ships around the globe.

1902

Charlie Woodward opens a department store in Vancouver, BC, and in 1926 he opens another Woodward's in Edmonton, Alberta. Woodward emulates the Eaton's stores and establishes a mail order business and is soon opening more stores. In 1993, suffering the effects of the 1980s economic recession, Woodward's declares bankruptcy and the name and some assets are acquired by the Hudson's Bay Company. Defunct for many years, there are now plans in the works to revive the company that so many remember with affection: Charlie Woodward's wonderful department stores.

1907

The Meat and Canned Food Act becomes law, enabling federal inspection of meat-packing plants. Canadians stop dying from bacteria-infected meats.

1909

George Saunders, a federal government cerealist, hybridizes a cold-tolerant, disease-resistant wheat called Marquis that sees distribution to all prairie farmers. In a decade, Saunders' discovery accounts for 90 percent of Canada's wheat crop.

1910

Arthur Ganong, a St. Stephen, New Brunswick, chocolate maker, has an idea that fishermen might like a convenient form of his product and invents the chocolate bar. The company, Ganong Bros. Limited, somehow having avoided conglomerate takeover, is producing candy in St. Stephen to this day and remains an all-Canadian family business.

1914

World War I begins, and Canadians learn the meaning of food rationing. Men with green thumbs build victory gardens, kids collect metal, grandmothers knit army socks, domestic servants disappear into munitions factories and moms across the nation create new ration-extending recipes and learn to bake barley bread.

1916

An American emigrant to Labrador, Clarence Birdseye, notices that fish caught and quickly frozen in barrels of seawater by local Innu people retain their freshness and flavour. He hatches a plan to commercialize the process and begins designing a plate and belt freezing system. In 1918, Birdseye returns to the U.S. to help in the war effort, and by 1924, he has his freezing technique perfected, and frozen fish fillets and vegetables are on the market.

In Canada, around 53 herbaceous plants are food crops (a mushroom and around 52 seed plants). The problem is, they all ripen during the warmer months. Clarence Birdseye's Labrador idea enables access to almost fresh veggies all winter long and provides a larger market for growers. However, at the time, there is no way for storekeepers to stock frozen products, so Birdseye gets to work and invents a freezer that will suit both the public and storekeepers. He even designs an electric light assembly to illuminate the front windows of stores that sell his frozen foods.

In 1929, Clarence Birdseye, called the Father of Frozen Foods, sold his patents to a company that would eventually become General Foods. When asked about his invention, Birdseye always credited the Innu people of Labrador for supplying the idea that changed cooking and eating habits around the world.

1918

The first rock salt mine in the British Commonwealth opens at Malagash, Nova Scotia. Already-cheap salt cod becomes even cheaper, dozens of new processing plants open and the die is cast for the eventual demise of the fishery.

1919

Theodore Pringle Loblaw opens Canada's first self-serve groceteria in Toronto and within a decade has 80 stores in Ontario and the American states of New York and Pennsylvania.

1920

J.L. Kraft, born in Stevensville, Ontario, adds a Montreal cheese factory to his burgeoning U.S. food-processing empire and gives his homeland a taste of his patented processed cheese.

1929

The Great Depression is not a market crash in Canada; economic collapse has been creeping up for a decade. In the West, successive years of severe drought and low grain prices have slowly leached the economic lifeblood from every prairie province, forcing 66 percent of the rural population onto relief. In British Columbia, the government has simply overspent the province into bankruptcy. In the Maritimes, the provinces have been broke since before 1929, when the downward spiral of the American stock market signalled the beginning of three extremely hard years. One-third of Canada's labour force is unemployed for those years, and one in five citizens depends on government relief for survival. Hard times have a profound effect on the nation's eating habits, and Sunday dinners spiral down from roast beef, to casserole, to creamed salmon on toast, to liver loaf with ketchup.

1930

Wonder Bread, the nation's first sliced and packaged bread, finds its way onto grocery store shelves. It was a 1921 innovation of the Taggert Baking Company of Indianapolis, Indiana, and named by that company's vice-president, Elmer Cline, who, after attending a hot air balloon race, said he had gazed in wonder at those balloons, and the word *wonder* had simply jumped from his yeast-soaked mind. Bought by Continental Bakeries in 1925, the Wonder brand was licensed to George Weston's Canada Bread in 1929 and remains the one of largest-selling breads in Canada.

1935

The Domestic Wine and Byproducts Company in British Columbia's Okanagan Valley changes its name to Calona Wines and switches production from apple to grape wines.

1937

Kraft Dinners appear on grocery store shelves.

1939

Canada is once again at war; men sign up to fight, and women leave their kitchens to join the armed services or work in factories. Manufactured foods that can be speedily prepared become an intrinsic part of wartime family meals. Canadian cuisine goes into overdrive and new recipes speed up the delivery of meals from oven to table.

1940

Fred Moffat, an electrical researcher employed by Canadian General Electric, invents the electric kettle, and meal preparations become even speedier.

1942

Food rationing becomes law, and Canadian families tighten their belts.

A brief summary about rationing, by Mary F. Williamson, extracted from letters written to her mother during World War II.

Another big problem, as far as imported foods were concerned, such as vegetables, oranges and other fresh fruits, was that access to U.S. currency was severely restricted. Canned foods became very scarce as much of what was available was being sent to the troops. Sugar rationing—the first food to be rationed—began on January 26, 1942, with ¾ lb. per week per person. The amount was reduced in April to ½ lb., and at the same time tea and coffee rationing began. It was still "voluntary rationing"; the books of ration stamps were introduced in June of 1942. But already meat was hard to find. A 20 percent tax was levied on sweets and voluntary rationing was extended to bacon, pork and cheese. By August, tea and coffee were on the formal ration list: a mere 1 oz. per week per person! Butter rationing began in late December, with an allowance of ½ lb. per week per person. Meat was put on the ration list in May of 1943 at 2 lb. per week per person. Consumers were complaining that little could be found in the shops; most pork was being sent overseas. During summer 1943, the prices of local fruits rocketed, but more sugar was permitted to households for preserving and bottling. In September, store-bought jams and jellies were rationed. Food shortages of all kinds persisted through 1943. It was certainly difficult to plan a traditional Christmas dinner. Unless you were prepared to canvas every store in your wider neighbourhood, many of the basics were unobtainable.

1944

American ex-serviceman William L. Maxson invents three-part frozen dinners for the U.S. military and calls them Stratoplates.

1945

Canadian servicemen and women involved in the Italian campaigns return from the war with a taste for an Italian food specialty called…pizza.

1946

American scientist Percy Spencer accidentally discovers that microwaves will cook food when a radio transmitter he is perfecting melts a candy bar on his worktable. His messy "eureka" moment will have far-reaching effects on the Canadian food experience.

1947

Kraft Foods tests the effectiveness of television advertising by reintroducing a defunct cheese brand called MacLaren's Imperial. Packed into a red cardboard container, the cheese is a huge success and marks the beginning of nationwide media campaigns by food processors to convince the public that industry-produced food is the modern, safer way to get dinner on the table.

1948

The Liberal government under Louis St. Laurent removes all barriers to U.S. investment and unofficially recognizes U.S. financial sovereignty.

1952

Our first television station, the CBC, begins broadcasting in Toronto and Montreal, and one of the first commercial advertisers is the Campbell Soup Company.

1954

The Saputo family, recently immigrated to Montreal from Italy, turn to making cheeses for the Italian community. In 1957, capitalizing on the rising popularity of pizza, they establish a factory to meet the demands of Quebec pizzerias. During the 1970s, Saputo expands production to meet the demands of pizzerias across the nation and enters the retail market. During the 1980s, Saputo expands into whey processing and the production of more varieties of cheese. In the 1990s, Saputo grows ever larger, acquires more companies, goes public and enters the new millennium as a home-grown food conglomerate.

1956

Loblaw Groceterias begin selling TV Dinner Brand Frozen Dinner, a C.A. Swanson product. In 1962, the company removes the "TV Dinner" brand from all their packaging and uses just the Swanson name. The name is still synonymous with frozen dinners.

1957

McCain Foods Limited opens a plant in Florenceville, New Brunswick, to process potatoes into frozen French fries. By the start of the new millennium, McCain is a global processor of potatoes with 30 factories located around the world.

1959

The St. Lawrence Seaway opens, enabling direct to the world wheat shipping from the lake head. The seaway also allows in the lamprey eel and hastens the demise of the Great Lakes fisheries.

1962

Edward Asselbergs, a research scientist at the Canadian Department of Agriculture in Ottawa, invents instant mashed potato flakes.

1964

Hockey great Tim Horton opens a doughnut shop in Hamilton, Ontario, and the national dementia of the Great Canadian Food Experience accelerates—fried flour breakfasts, fried flour and meat lunches, and dinner served on aluminium trays while watching television.

1967

American fast food impresario Ray Kroc takes his rapidly expanding McDonald's hamburger franchise international with a restaurant in Richmond, BC.

1976

Dr. Helmut Becker of Germany's famed Geisenheim Wine Institute supplies BC's Okanagan wine growers with 27 varieties of grape vines for trials that will establish the base varietals for the fast-maturing Okanagan wine industry.

1980

M&M Meat Shops opens a store in Kitchener, Ontario, to sell boxed frozen meats to consumers wary of conglomerate meat packers. Today, M&M has almost 500 stores across the nation, with their boxed meat products offering consumers a way to distance themselves from the abattoirs.

1987

Canada and the U.S. sign a free trade agreement that unhinges all manner of Canadian food conspiracies and increases our dependence on the U.S. in both exports and imports. Faced with competition from the U.S., Canadian meat-packing plants merge, and farmers are forced into growing quality rather than weight. Canadian consumers benefit, but control of food production slips away as more processing companies are bought out by U.S. conglomerates.

1990

British-controlled Canada Packers and Maple Leaf Mills merge to become a mega conglomerate called Maple Leaf Foods.

1994

A tomato called Flavr Savr, the first genetically modified food, appears in supermarkets, quickly followed by corn, strawberries and potatoes. By the end of the century, almost 70 percent of our agricultural output is genetically altered, and food allergies are on the rise.

1995

Ex-CEO of McCain Foods, Wallace McCain, and the Ontario Teachers Pension Plan buy Maple Leaf Foods from the British and create Canada's very own mega food conglomerate—bleat, bawl, oink, freeze or fry, the McCain boys have it covered.

1996

Food Network, a start-up culinary TV channel, becomes popular in the U.S. and in Canada as an imported cable channel. In 2000, Alliance Atlantis Corporation launches Food Network Canada, and while some programming focuses on Canadian cuisine, the majority is concerned with what's cooking in other places.

2001

The Italian mega food conglomerate Parmalat, owner of the Beatrice, Sealtest, Lancantia, Balderson, Black Diamond and Astro brands, withdraws from membership in the National Dairy Council of Canada, effectively destroying that agency and leaving small dairies without government representation.

2008

Maple Leaf Foods meat products are found contaminated by the listeria bacteria and are subject to a massive recall. Listeria contamination found in other food-processing plants across the nation causes consumers to lose confidence in conglomerate-produced foods. Sales of organic and farm gate foods skyrocket.

Home gardens proliferate, and stores are hard-pressed to keep up with demand for Mason canning jars.

2009

Wal-Mart stores across Canada begin stocking organic foods, and the word "locovore," meaning food grown and consumed locally, enters our vocabulary.

2010

An oil rig off the coast of Louisiana explodes on April 20, killing 11 people and causing a massive oil leak in the Gulf of Mexico. The oil spill will negatively impact the environment for years to come, including placing a strain on fish and shellfish populations. Officials with the Canadian government assure us that strict Canadian safety rules will prevent such a disaster from ever happening in our waters…we can only hope they're right.

There you have it, the entire history of Canadian cuisine. By 2010 Canadian kitchens have gone from hard work and hearths to rarely used stainless steel appliances and granite countertops; ingredients are not foraged from the forest but are flown in from faraway places; carefully hoarded recipes are replaced by the internet and Food TV-created internationally famous chefs; and fast food restaurants are being pressed into providing nutritional content of their menu items for people who are still too stressed out to learn to cook with their stainless steel appliances.

But there is a light at the end of the tunnel. People are discovering gardening—there is a virtual edible gardening revolution—and from gardens comes greatness in cuisine. Pick up a hoe, folks, and dig in.

Encyclopedia of Canadian Cuisine

Many tried and true, along with plenty fresh and new.

A

ACORN COFFEE—brewed by the very desperate from roasted and ground seeds or nuts of various oak trees native to Canada, the most common being the bur oak (*Quercus macrocarpa*).

ALBERTA BEEF RIBS—a delicious culinary conjuration of old-time Alberta chuckwagon cooks that in modern times has become a staple offering of dude ranches, upscale western steakhouses and your kitchen once you try the recipe.

RECIPE

Alberta Beef Ribs

Brown beef ribs on all sides in a Dutch oven. Pour on a seasoned stew of chopped onions, carrots, celery, canned tomatoes, wild or Dijon mustard, honey and garlic, and hot sauce if you like it; cook for 3–4 hours. To turn tasty into scrumptious, remove ribs after 3 hours, brush with honey and wild mustard and finish on the barbecue.

A

TRIVIA

Alberta Beef

- Almost 6 million head of cattle graze Alberta's foothills, and no better place exists to make them happy. Alberta beef cattle eat the finest grass, drink the purest water and, when the time comes for a little marbling, get to munch the world's best grain. To paraphrase Food TV's Alton Brown, "Happy cows make...Good Eats."

- Alberta's 36,000 producers export over $1 billion worth of good eats around the globe.

ALEWIFE (*Alosa pseudoharengus*; also called spring herring, gaspereau, kiak)—a member of the herring family, this small (10–30 cm long), rough-scaled fish takes to curing by salt readily, and during the 1800s, millions of the little fish were salt-pickled into barrels and shipped abroad, while millions more saw use as fish bait or fertilizer. Cheap and always plentiful, the alewife became the main ingredient of hundreds of different recipes.

TRIVIA

Alewife

- Today, adult alewives are the preferred bait for lobster fishermen, and a small industry has sprung up canning alewife eggs, or roe. The remainder of the catch is smoked, pickled, used in pet food or made into fishmeal.

- Alewives introduced into Pacific rivers now range from California to Alaska and have become a vital food resource for depleted salmon stocks.

- The alewife earned its name from having a pronounced belly reminiscent of those found on overindulgent wives of tavern owners.

A

ALEWIFE

As an indicator of the size and importance of the mid-1800s alewife fishery, records from this period show over 35,000 barrels of salt-pickled alewives shipped from Nova Scotia and New Brunswick annually. Nowadays, alewives are still pickled, but a pail has replaced the barrel, and shipping is to the Middle East and the Caribbean. Thin and bony, so not as prized as regular herring, the fish made up for those shortcomings by ease of procurement and sheer numbers. Alewives breed and spawn in fresh water, making their appearance in major river systems around the beginning of May. In earlier times, alewives would move into the rivers in such numbers that simple seine nets laid across constrictions enabled a thriving commercial trade. While a commercial fishery still exists today, primarily from rivers feeding the southern Gulf of St. Lawrence and Bay of Fundy, it is not thriving owing to overfishing and degradation of breeding habitats. Alewives readily adapt to freshwater living and can be landlocked in lakes, especially those comprising the Great Lakes system. Overfishing and lamprey predation of native fish stocks during the 1950s led to a dramatic rise in Great Lakes alewife populations until the introduction of predator salmon species and aggressive culling of invasive lamprey eels brought their numbers back under control.

AMERICAN CHESTNUT. *See* chestnut.

AMERICAN SHAD. *See* shad.

AN EXCELLENT CAKE—recipe #146 in *The Cook Not Mad*, a very rich cake from those good ol' days when waistline was hardly a word.

A

RECIPE

An Excellent Cake

Mix 2 lbs flour, 1 lb butter, 1 teacup of yeast with warm milk and set it to rise. Add 2 lbs currants, 1 lb sugar, ¼ lb almonds, ½ lb raisins chopped fine, 1 tsp each nutmeg, cinnamon and cloves, a peel of lemon chopped fine, a glass each of wine and brandy, 12 eggs (yolks and whites beaten separately and thoroughly) and the juice of 1 orange and 1 lemon, and pop into a 375° F oven until a pick comes out clean, 30–40 minutes. Whew! Reads like an American extravaganza.

TRIVIA

Cookbooks

The Cook Not Mad (1831) was Canada's first cookbook. It became a bestseller and mainstay kitchen guidebook for Canadian housewives. Only later was it discovered that the publisher, James Macfarlane of Kingston, had plagiarized almost the entire book, including the title, from the American publisher Knowlton and Rice, of Watertown, New York, 60 kilometres from Kingston. Was it outright theft or hoax, or had Macfarlane merely demonstrated how Canadians can be easily fooled by those words "made in Canada"? Nobody knows, but since he owned the Kingston newspaper and never advertised the cookbook, one must surmise a warning—Canada should stand apart from the U.S. and promote its own heritage.

ANADAMA BREAD—iconic east coast cornmeal yeast bread sweetened with molasses. A favourite of fishermen, this richly flavoured bread is also made with whole-wheat flour. *See also* bread.

A

APPLE (*Malus domestica*)—Pomme-gris, Fameuse (snow apple), Canada-red, St. Lawrence, Canada Reinette, McIntosh, Baldwin, Spy, Cortland, Gravenstein, Cox, Jonathan, and the list goes on and on— there are thousands of apple varieties. Apple trees are good at remembering friends and relatives, and planting a seed of one variety may produce a tree of a different variety. To avoid this biological idiosyncrasy, orchard-grown apple trees are always grafted stock: the wood of a desired tree is surgically attached to the roots of trees well suited to area growing  conditions. The McIntosh apples you purchase from a supermarket all come from grafts of the original tree discovered by John McIntosh in 1813, near Peterborough, Ontario.

APPLE AND WILD RICE—a First Nations favourite of crabapples and wild rice; quickly adapted by pioneer families with access to hybrid, European-style apples. Still popular today, the tasty combination makes a wonderful salad or stuffing for wild or domestic fowl.

A

TRIVIA

Apples

• Apple trees are not native to Canada, and while we did have two native crabapples much used by First Nations, those trees provided only famine food to settlers as they waited for seeds they brought from home to mature. First Nations jumped at the chance to acquire European apple varieties, and settlers were often surprised to find apple trees had preceded them to new areas.

• Every decade or so, a new apple variety makes an appearance at local farmers' markets. New apples are a big hit in their area, but seldom, if ever, make the jump to national distribution, as doing so would disturb the status quo of tree to market distribution. However, there are occasional exceptions, and a BC-grown apple called Ambrosia is currently wending its way into the national food experience. Keep your eyes peeled, and if you spot this beauty anywhere, grab a few and prepare for a taste sensation.

• Once a major player in the international apple market, Canada's world market share has shrunk considerably, and we are now only the 16th largest apple producing country—but just wait until the world tastes an Ambrosia apple.

APPLE BUTTER—a hard, cooked-until-thick, spiced applesauce condiment popular from the very earliest times and made wherever apples grew. While not originally Canadian, as the recipe was brought by either English or German settlers, apple butter has been naturalized over many generations by the use of Canadian apples.

APPLE CIDER—an easy-to-make alcoholic beverage produced by fermenting apple juice in a closed container equipped with a one-way valve. No sugar or yeasts are needed, and after a few

A

weeks of fermentation, the party can begin. Apple cider has been a Canadian treat since the 16th century and is traditionally pressed from windfall apples (ripe apples picked from the ground after storms). Artisanal cider presses are located in most Canadian provinces; the largest, Growers Cider Company in Victoria, BC, markets ciders across the nation.

APPLE CIDER BRANDY—a high-proof distillation of apple cider, and a backyard specialty of many apple growers from pioneer days to the present. In BC and Quebec, several artisanal distilleries are engaged in the legal production of cider brandy.

APPLE CIDER VINEGAR—an easy-to-make, extremely good vinegar produced by the fermentation of apple juice in an open container.

APPLE MOLASSES (also called apple syrup)—a staple sweetener of pioneer settlers; still popular with today's discerning chefs. Apple molasses or syrup is used to sweeten cereal, to drizzle over pancakes and in any recipe calling for molasses. Made from fresh cider boiled to syrup, apple molasses, usually labelled as apple syrup, is available in some supermarkets and fine food stores.

APPLE SCHNAPPS—an *eau-de-vie* once produced by many backyard distillers, but today the best legal production in Canada comes from the stills of Winegarden Estates in Baie-Verte, New Brunswick, and the Rodrigues family winery in Markland, Newfoundland. Both firms turn apples into liquor so crisp and clean it will leave you breathless and wondering why you can only buy it in those provinces.

APPLE SNOW PUDDING—an unpeeled applesauce dessert made by beating rosy-coloured sauce into whipped egg whites while adding sugar and powdered ginger root. Easy to make, this classic east coast favourite has become a darling of upscale chefs and is widely used to finish classic Canadian meals.

A

APPLE SOUP—popular then and now, apples work wonderfully in combination with various vegetables such as parsnips, turnips, potatoes and squash.

APPLE SYRUP. *See* apple molasses.

APPLE TAPIOCA—an abundance of apples prompted early settlers to use them in inventive ways, especially in sweet deserts.

RECIPE

Apple Tapioca

Mix ½ cup softened tapioca with 6 peeled, cored and sliced cooking apples in a baking dish. Bake for ½ hour at 375° F. Add a pinch of salt, ¾ cup sugar, 2 tsp lemon juice and a shot of cinnamon. Stir and then bake for another 20 minutes. Cool and serve with thick or whipped cream.

APPLEJACK—an easy-to-make but crude pioneer whisky made only in the winter months. Fill an outside barrel with hard cider and remove the ice as it freezes. Alcohol does not freeze and will separate from the water, and when the parting of the ways is complete, the party can begin.

APPLESAUCE—a purée made from cooked apples and a favourite condiment and dessert of both pioneer and modern families. Sweet or unsweetened applesauce made from fresh picked apples is a culinary delight best consumed immediately—a few days in the fridge will have it tasting like the ubiquitous canned version.

APPLESAUCE CAKE—a favourite of early settlers and still going strong, this delicious cake uses no eggs and relies on applesauce for its light, moist texture.

ARCTIC CHAR (*Salvelinus alpinus*)—a member of the Salmon family, but with a milder taste and tiny scales. Native to arctic

A

and subarctic streams and lakes, char has a most agreeable flavour and may be prepared in dozens of ways.

ARCTIC GRAYLING (*Thymallus arcticus*)—related to trout and whitefish, grayling are native to rivers and lakes of northern BC, NWT and Alberta. A popular game fish, the flesh is white, flaky and bland.

ASPARAGUS CASSEROLE—a springtime favourite of Canada West settlers, this Cheddar cheese and fresh asparagus delight is still going strong. Asparagus casserole is a scrumptious side dish for baked ham.

RECIPE

Asparagus Casserole

Cover 2–3 lbs fresh asparagus spears with Cheddar cheese sauce (find a recipe online), top with a mixture of bread crumbs and butter, and bake for 20–25 minutes at 350° F.

TRIVIA

Asparagus

According to trials conducted in England, a Canadian asparagus variety bred at the University of Guelph and called Guelph Millennium is the world's best-growing and finest-tasting asparagus.

A

ATLANTIC HERRING (*Clupea harengus*; also called sardine, brisling, sprat, pilchard)—a small Atlantic schooling fish consumed by almost everything that moves on, over or in the ocean. Herring are the dominant fish species in our east coast waters and are available fresh, frozen, smoked or canned.

ATLANTIC MACKEREL. *See* mackerel.

AVONLEA CHEDDAR CHEESE—artisanal PEI cow's milk Cheddar wrapped in cloth to preserve moisture during the aging process…sensational.

AYLMER CANNED TOMATOES—a favourite of Canadians since Aylmer, Ontario, residents David Marshall and Thomas Nairn established the company in 1881. Southwestern Ontario is one of the world's great tomato-growing areas, and despite being owned by the U.S. investment company Sun Capital Partners, Aylmer still manages to get the best of our crop into cans.

B

BACALAO—a Newfoundland and Portuguese culinary marvel made from dried salt cod. There are at least 100 recipes. Bacalao is the Portuguese word for salt cod and quite possibly their 16th-century name for where the dish originated: Newfoundland.

RECIPE

Tomato Sauce Bacalao

Fry 2 lbs desalted and floured cod both sides in ¼ cup olive oil and set aside. Add ½ cup olive oil to pan along with 1 chopped onion and 3 cloves chopped garlic; sauté until translucent. Add a 28 oz tin of crushed tomatoes and 1 bay leaf; simmer 10 minutes. Add fish along with a 12 oz jar of roasted red peppers; cover and simmer 5 minutes. Serve with fried potatoes.

BACALAO

Jenaro Pildain, owner and chef of Gurai, a famous bacalao restaurant in Bilboa, Spain, recommends soaking salt cod for 36 hours with four water changes and a final soak in mineral water to remove any chlorine taste from the tap water. Other great bacalao chefs recommend a longer soak, up to 48 hours, but somewhere in between should suffice to desalt and plump the fish for your bacalao.

B

BACHELOR BUTTON COOKIES—a buttery favourite of pioneer bakers because the recipe called for no soda. Bachelor buttons were a special favourite on the Prairies and were always included in the overseas Christmas packages sent to Canadian forces fighting on the battlefields of World War I.

BACK BACON—Canadian-style bacon, a cured and smoked bacon cut from pork loin. Roasted back bacon was a favourite meal of settlers in early fall when hogs were butchered. Nowadays, it is mostly served as a breakfast side, or paired with poached eggs and Hollandaise sauce on English muffins in a dish called Eggs Benedict.

BACON AND APPLE TOAST—apples stewed with butter and sugar and piled onto slices of thick, butter-fried bread layered with crispy bacon.

BAGEL AND NOVA LOX—a Montreal-style sliced bagel slathered with cream cheese and topped with slices of cold or hot smoked Nova Scotia salmon.

BAKEAPPLE JAM—a delicious jam made from the yellow drupes (berries) of the bakeapple plant (*Rubus chamaemorus*; called cloudberry in other parts of the world). The jam is a favourite on the east coast, especially in Newfoundland. Bakeapple berries are also used to make scrumptious pies, puddings and jellies.

BAKED BEANS—a dried pea or navy bean casserole; one of the iconic foods of Canadian cuisine.

B

RECIPE

Classic Canadian Baked Beans

Boil 2 cups navy beans for 2 minutes and set aside overnight. Drain liquid and replace with 5 cups hot water. Add 2 tsp each dry mustard and salt, and ¼ tsp pepper. Simmer for 1 hour on stovetop. Transfer beans and liquid to iron pot. Add ¼ lb salt pork, 1 sliced onion, ¼ cup maple sugar, 3 Tbsp maple syrup and 2 Tbsp molasses. Cover and bake for 5 hours, adding water if beans become dry.

BAKED BEANS

Hundreds of recipe variations exist for baked beans—sweet, slightly sweet, unsweetened, spicy, plain, with or without salt pork, beef, venison—but all are rooted in the original one pot, the extremely boring ship's kettle of beans. In the 16th century, fishing fleets headed for the New World were provisioned by sensible, unimaginative men with dried peas, beans, salt pork, hardtack and salt, all in barrels, along with a large iron kettle to cook the salt pork and beans. However, those 16th-century sailors were an imaginative lot, and they seized upon any opportunity to elevate the palatability of their beans. Their first contact with indigenous people, the Mi'kmaq, would have provided sailors with maple syrup, wild garlic and a haunch or two of venison. All went into the ship's bean pot, and life suddenly got a whole lot better for those homesick sailors.

B

Baked Beans

Jacques Cartier had traded with the Mi'kmaq on his first voyage to the New World in 1534, according to a note in his ship's log. Although no record exists as to what goods changed hands, food must have been tantamount, and that meant the bean pot. Pork and beans with onions and sweetener *and* in 1534—almost a century before any Puritan set foot in a place called Boston, and two centuries before anyone thought of adding tomato sauce.

BAKED CUSTARD—a silky smooth, baked egg and milk pudding happily consumed by generations of Canadian children and made even better with a dollop of whipped cream and a few scrapes of nutmeg.

RECIPE

Baked Custard

Scald 2 cups milk. Beat together 3 eggs, ¼ cup sugar and ¼ tsp salt and add slowly to milk. Add 1 tsp vanilla. Pour into ramekins or a dish and bake in a bain marie *(water bath) at 350° F for 1 hour, or until a knife comes out clean.*

BAKED KETTLE BREAD—bread baked in an iron Dutch oven (the baking kettle), which was either hung from a hearth crane or set upon hot coals with some more coals piled on the lid. *See also* bread.

BAKED TURR—turr is a sea bird, true name murre (*Urai aalge*), but called turr in Newfoundland. The birds are skinned, baked like small chickens and very popular—around 15,000 hunters are licensed to hunt the birds.

BAKER'S CHEESE. *See* hoop cheese.

BALDERSON CHEDDAR CHEESE—established in 1881 at Balderson Corners, Ontario, Balderson produces prize-winning aged Cheddars despite being owned by the mighty Italian-based food conglomerate Parmalat.

B

BALSAMROOT BREAD—a west coast specialty bread enjoyed by coastal First Nations and newly arrived settlers and made from a flour of pounded balsamroot (*Balsamorhiza sagittata*), a flowering perennial native to BC. *See also* bread.

BANGBELLY—a Newfoundland fried pancake made from flour, water, baking soda, molasses, a pinch of salt and pork fat.

BANNOCK—originally a simple bread of Scottish origin, bannock saw adaptation by Canadian voyageurs, fur trappers and First Nations as an unleavened hearth cake made from a rudimentary dough of Indian meal, water, fat and a pinch of salt. Much improved with the advent of baking soda, bannock has become the iconic bread of the Canadian North.

RECIPE

Bannock

Mix 6 cups flour, 1 cup lard, 3 Tbsp baking powder, 1 Tbsp salt and 3½ cups water into a dough. Knead for a bit, flatten into cakes and bake on a hot rock or in the oven until brown. Adding a handful of raisins will considerably improve the bread.

B

BARLEY BREAD—although called barley bread, the dough is actually a mixture of wheat and barley flours. Inclusion of the latter is meant to cheapen the cost of the bread. *See also* bread.

TRIVIA

Barley

• Canada is second only to Russia in barley production, with most going to feed cattle and supply the brewing and distilling industries.

• Barley is more nutritious than wheat but contains a starch that is incompatible with wheat in the milling process; however, a Canadian hybridized barley called Millhouse will soon allow millers to mix the two, producing a healthier, ready mixed flour for bread making.

BARLEY TOY CANDY—a clear, barley sugar candy moulded into dozens of different candy toys by the Robertson Candy Company of Truro, Nova Scotia, since 1928. Originally made as Christmas tree decorations, the candy toys in hundreds of different shapes have become a festive favourite of Maritimers. Robertson Candy also makes another east coast holiday favourite, the Satin Mix ribbon candy, and many other chocolate and sugar creations.

BARLEY SUGAR

Barley sugar is barley water boiled with cream of tarter and refined sugar. Barley water is a nutritious decoction, or soup, of pearl barley. Barley water mixed with fruit juice is a popular English beverage and an ingredient in the manufacture of hard candies.

BARLEY WINE—a top fermented beer (ale) with alcohol content similar to wine. Brewed by early settlers, the beer is still produced by seven or eight artisanal breweries across Canada.

B

BARM—yeast formed on malt liquors during the brewing or distilling process, the froth; the source of a rudimentary yeast once used for bread rising.

BARMY BREAD—any bread using barm for rising; a word used to describe already risen bread.

BASSWOOD TEA. *See* linden tea.

BATTERCAKE. *See* corn oyster.

BAY SALMON. *See* salmon.

BEAKED HAZELNUTS. *See* hazelnuts.

BEAN PORRIDGE—originally a Scottish breakfast food made with split green peas—peas porridge—the dish became Canadian when early settlers substituted beans for peas.

BEAR STEW—a one-pot favourite of First Nations, early Canadian settlers and modern hunters. Aside from marinating cubed bear meat for 24 hours, the stew is prepared following a regular recipe.

B

Bears

In Canada, sportsmen and First Nations hunters harvest around 20,000 bears annually. In pioneer days, young bears were hunted for both meat and fat, the latter rendered down to make lard for pastry.

BEARBERRY JAM. *See* buffaloberry jam.

BEARBERRY POPCORN. *See* buffaloberry popcorn.

BEAVER TAILS (also called *queues de castors*)—once a baked, waste-not-want-not delicacy enjoyed by First Nations and fur trappers, the words have evolved to mean a fried slab of risen dough dusted with cinnamon and sugar or any number of toppings. Trademarked by Pam and Grant Hooker and first served at Ottawa's Byward Market, the tails have become uniquely Canadian and a real treat for small fry. *See also* dough gods.

BEECHNUT COFFEE—roasted and ground beechnuts served as a passable coffee imitation for desperate-for-a-fix pioneers, but beechnuts were more often gathered and pressed for oil or roasted as a snack food.

BEECHNUT TREES

Beechnut trees were plentiful in pioneer days, and the nuts were easily harvested since they fall from the tree when ripe. Today, foragers gather beechnuts, but owing to the trees' extreme suitability as firewood, the number of trees has diminished considerably.

BEECHNUT COOKIES—iconic Canadian pioneer cookie baked every fall when beechnut trees became heavily loaded with the prickly nut husks.

B

RECIPE

Beechnut Cookies

Remove enough nuts from their husks to fill a 4 cup container and toast in frypan or oven. Cream 1 cup sugar with ½ cup shortening; add 4 egg yolks and the juice from ½ lemon. Sift 2 cups flour with 3 tsp baking powder and 1 tsp salt and mix with ½ cup milk. Add toasted nuts, spoon onto greased tin and bake at 350° F for 10 minutes or until golden.

BEECHNUT OIL—for many pioneer families, the nuts of beechnut trees found in the forests of eastern and central Canada were a principal source of cooking and lamp oil.

BEER—almost every pioneer farmer grew barley and made cottage-style or home brew, but it was the British army that caused commercial breweries to spring up in almost every town and village. Ale is the tradition on the east coast; Belgium-style beers lead the parade in Quebec; lagers win in Ontario; and pilsners are the preferred quaff of prairie dwellers and folks in BC.

BEER

To keep British troops in lonely postings required some bribery, and for the British army in Canada that included a daily ration of six pints of beer. To supply the sudsy elixir, the British army imported brewmasters and set up breweries. The ensuing and ongoing party saw lots of beer drunk by lots of rough men who only cared what it did and not how it tasted. However, as time went on people who did care about taste arrived in Canada, prompting

B

people like Canada's greatest entrepreneur, John Molson, to produce quality as well as quantity. Molson started up his brewery in 1786 and never looked back, and by the time he passed away in 1836 he was making ale and running banks for all of Lower Canada.

In 1818, a London, Ontario (then Canada West), farmer named John Carling began pushing beer out his back door and down the streets of London in a wheelbarrow. By 1840 he had established a brewery in that city and was topping up beer mugs from muddy York to Windsor.

In 1862, Eugene O'Keefe bought a brewery in York (now Toronto) and began making Canada's first lager beer.

In 1867, Susanna Oland began brewing a quality beer in the backyard of her home in Dartmouth, Nova Scotia, and within a few years was brewing quality beer for the eastern part of the country.

On the Prairies and west to the coast, many breweries started up around 1883, but in the formative years of the 20th century, most were controlled by an American, Fritz Sick. By 1930, he and his son were making pilsner and knocking heads with Molson, O'Keefe and Carling for market share. Big bought little all across Canada, and by the century's end, big ruled market share until eaten up by foreign-owned conglomerates.

What goes around comes around, and as the 21st century progresses, small breweries called microbreweries are once again on the rise and producing all kinds of interesting brews for a thirsty public that consumes $4 billion worth of beer annually.

B

BEET MOLASSES—white beets, or sugar beets, contain a significant amount of sugar, and starting around the middle of the 19th century, pressed beet juice would be cooked down by Quebec settlers and farmers into molasses in a process similar to maple syrup production. Extensive planting of sugar beets in that province prompted the building of a beet

refinery in 1881 to produce regular sugar, and by 1902, four refineries were processing Ontario beets, with several more opening on the Prairies.

BEETROOT WINE—an easily made alcoholic beverage of fermented sugar beets. It was a one-time favourite of habitant farmers and home brewers.

BEIGNET—a puffy, deep-fried pastry of French origin naturalized by the addition of maple sugar: maple beignet.

BELLY BUSTERS—Alberta chuckwagon camp biscuits usually served with baked beans.

BERKSHIRE PORK—an English heritage breed of pig adopted by niche market Canadian pork producers who raise them by old-fashioned, ethical methods. Since there are more Berkshires in Canada than anywhere else, that makes them our special pig.

BERRY CAKE—an early pioneer emulation of a First Nations method of storing dried berries that in later years evolved into a cake topped with a fresh berry sauce.

BERRY FOOL—a dessert made with fresh berries folded into sweetened whipped cream.

BERRY WINE—any fermented alcoholic beverage made with wild or cultivated berries: elderberry, raspberry, blueberry, etc.

B

BICKS PICKLES—a national favourite since 1944, the year Jeanny and Walter Bick of Scarborough, Ontario, responded to a collapse of the cucumber market by turning tons of their field cucumbers into pickles. These good pickles caught the public's attention and launched the couple into the pickle business. The business prospered, and in 1966, the couple sold the business to Robin Hood Foods, now a part of the U.S. food conglomerate Smuckers.

BIG PANCAKE—a traditional Easter breakfast dish favoured by the people of the Charlevoix area of Quebec. It is an oversized egg, flour and baking soda pancake that is oven baked, drenched in maple syrup and accompanied by crisp salt pork or ham slices.

BIRCH SYRUP—the sweet boiled-down sap of almost any birch tree, but white birch (*Betula papyrifera*) is preferred. Sap is tapped from trees before buds set, or the syrup takes on a bitter taste. It also must be evaporated within  24 hours because the sap ferments quickly. Birch syrup is sometimes available at farmers' markets, and some commercial production occurs in Quebec.

BIRCH WINE—an alcoholic beverage made from the quickly fermenting sap of birch trees.

BIRD'S CUSTARD POWDER—invented in England by Alfred Bird in 1837 because his wife was allergic to eggs. The cornstarch-based pudding mix became popular around the globe and especially in Canada where, after 1843, Alfred Bird sent shiploads along with his newly invented baking powder. Around 1920, the company was purchased by Kraft Foods, and in 2004, Kraft sold it to Premier Foods, the owner of the Cadbury and Oxo brands. Available at supermarkets nationwide, Bird's Custard Powder is to some a necessary ingredient for making Nanaimo bars, while others prefer Horne's Custard Powder.

BISHOP'S PUDDING—a date and walnut cake with sauce from the Pointe Claire area of Quebec.

BISON CHUCKWAGON STEW—a one-pot bison meat and vegetable stew favoured by 19th-century Alberta cowboys.

BISON

Bison, or buffalo, were ubiquitous on the Canadian Prairies until the latter part of the 19th century, when market hunting almost obliterated the species. Today, thanks to ranchers setting aside sections of range land for bison grazing, bison numbers have risen to around a half million, and the animals are a valuable, sustainable source of revenue for ranchers.

TRIVIA

Bison

Two insurmountable problems hampered westward expansion of the U.S. and Canada during the early part of the 19th century: bison and First Nations. Fifty million bison made settlement impossible, and First Nations were (obviously) resisting appropriation of their lands, so both the U.S. and Canadian governments launched efforts to reduce both populations. Plains First Nations depended on bison for sustenance; the policy of "slaughter every animal and both problems would disappear" was carried out with vigour.

B

BISTORT (*Bistorta vivipara*)—a much-foraged perennial that grows at higher altitudes and belongs to the Buckwheat family. It was very familiar to Canada's early settlers because a similar variety grew in the home country. Peeled, the rhizomes may be eaten boiled or fresh and taste like almonds, while the leaves make a delicious salad green. Bistort seeds may be gathered and ground into bread flour, while the plant's tiny bulblets make a tasty snack.

BLACK CURRANT JAM—the absolute favourite jam of both early pioneers and modern foragers. The ripe berries are packed with so much pectin that any 10-year-old kid can make a batch of these preserves.

RECIPE

Black Currant Jam

Mix 2 cups ripe black currants with 1 cup each granulated sugar and water. Cook uncovered until berries are soft. Pour into sterilized jars, seal and keep in a cool place.

BLACK CURRANT SCHNAPPS—an old-time favourite of backyard distillers who used black currant syrup to dampen the flames of homemade hooch.

BLACK RIVER CHEESE—located in Milford, Ontario, Black River has been creating superlative cheeses since 1901 and is a consistent prize-winner at both the British Empire Cheese Competition and the Royal Winter Fair. Black River's emphasis is on aged Cheddar up to six years old, but they also produce fine mozzarella and goat's milk cheeses, including a fantastic sheep/cow's milk Cheddar—a shared effort with Fifth Town Artisan Cheese Company. Black River cheeses are widely available in Ontario, some national outlets and online.

BLACK TRUFFLE CHEDDAR—an outstanding cow's milk Cheddar crafted by Bothwell Cheese Inc. in New Bothwell, Manitoba, since 1936. This taste sensation, along with their other fine cheeses, is available nationwide and online.

BLACK WALNUT AND MAPLE COOKIES—a kitchen marvel that provided a culinary diversion to pioneer families trapped inside by winter's fury. Walnuts, flour, eggs, maple syrup, butter and a touch of salt worked magic in those log cabins, and with the addition of vanilla you'll think you're getting a taste of heaven.

BLACK WALNUT AND PUMPKIN SOUP—a favourite soup of First Nations and quickly adopted by early settlers.

RECIPE

Black Walnut and Pumpkin Soup

Bake a clean pumpkin until the flesh is soft, then scrape it off the rind and mash it in a saucepan with maple syrup, black walnuts and a pinch of salt. Add water to liquefy, simmer for 5 minutes and serve with a garnish of chopped walnuts.

BLACKBERRY TEA—a hot water infusion of dried leaves and or berries of the blackberry plant (*Rubus fruticosus*), a relative of the common raspberry and member of the Rose family.

BLACKBERRY WINE—an alcoholic beverage made from fermented blackberries, and a favourite of both early pioneers and modern day imbibers.

B

Blackberries

- Although native to northern North America, blackberries are widely cultivated in Mexico and are an important export crop. In those growing areas of Mexico that lack a winter chill to set buds, the canes are chemically defoliated and forced into bloom by application of chemical growth regulators. What's in your breakfast bowl?

- Although the roots of both blackberry and raspberry plants (*Rubus* spp.) are perennial, the canes are biennial, meaning they only survive for two years: the first for growing, and the second for setting buds.

- Blackberries, like raspberries, are not single fruits, but many drupelets gathered in clusters. When picked, blackberries come off whole, while raspberries leave their core and are hollow.

- Blackberries are an excellent source of the antioxidants known to combat the effects of old age and are becoming an increasingly important crop in British Columbia—the berry canes grow best in a temperate climate.

- Blackberry is the common name for a family of bush berries that includes dewberry, boysenberry and loganberry.

BLAZE'S BEANS—BC packed, pickled green beans—hot, spicy and perfect for stirring Bloody Caesars.

BLEU ERMITE CHEESE—a blue cheese from the Fromagerie de L'Abbaye Saint-Benoit, in St-Benoit-du-Lac, Quebec, a dairy owned and operated by Benedictine monks. Created in 1943 and exclusive to the brothers' Fromagerie, this cheese is available only in specialty cheese shops.

B

BLOODY CAESAR—a popular clam and tomato juice–based cocktail invented in 1969 by bartender Walter Chell at the Calgary Inn. The drink he called Bloody Caesar caught the attention of both the imbibing public and American apple juice magnet Duffy Mott. With Chell's help, Mott concocted a tomato and clam juice ready mix for the Bloody Caesar, calling it Clamato juice. It's an all-Canadian cocktail, and we quaff over 300 million of the tasty beverage every year.

BLUE CAMAS (*Camassia quamash*)—a perennial member of the Lily family and an important food source for west coast First Nations who cultivated the plant for its sweet, potato-like root. Camas roots contain significant amounts of the complex sugar inulin, which, when heated slowly in steam pits, converts to almost half the root's weight in fructose sugar. Although a good source of sweetener, blue camas never saw adoption by Europeans because it closely resembles an extremely poisonous plant species called death camas. Even First Nations harvesters always waited for the blue camas to flower before digging up the bulbs.

BLUE COD. *See* ling cod.

BLUE MONDAY CAKE. *See* wacky cake.

BLUE MUSSELS. *See* mussels.

B

BLUEBERRY BUCKLE—a blueberry pudding or fruitcake favoured by pioneer families at berry-gathering time. Made more popular with the advent of baking soda, the lighter version of blueberry buckle is still enjoyed by Canadians from coast to coast.

TRIVIA

Blueberries

- In 1996, blueberries supplanted apples as the number one fruit crop in Canada in terms of area. Total production surpasses 70,000 tons, with most of that quantity destined for export. Of that amount, about half is wild, or low bush blueberry, grown in the Maritimes, and the rest is the highbush variety grown in BC. Canada accounts for about half of the world production of wild blueberries.

- Blueberries contain significant amounts of anthocyanins, antioxidants and photochemicals that offer protection from cancer and various diseases of old age. A swig of blueberry juice every day will keep the doctor away.

BLUEBERRY CHUTNEY—a condiment originating in British-ruled India but Canadianized by substituting fresh blueberries for mangos.

BLUEBERRY GRUNT—a potpie, or cobbler, made by filling a large iron pot with berries, with or without sugar, topping it with biscuit dough and cooking it over a fire. The name comes from the sound steam makes when escaping the pot. *See also* fungy.

BLUEBERRY PIE—dessert pie filled with berries iconic to Canadian culinary history. First Nations munched the berries, the Vikings fermented them, the French made sauce and the English made cobbler, but it was the Acadians who put the berries into a pastry crust and gave us blueberry pie, albeit in a crust probably made with rendered bear fat.

B

BLUEBERRY SAUCE—First Nations were spooning blueberry sauce onto roast game long before settlers arrived in Canada. Every season they harvested huge quantities of the delectable berries, dried them in sunshine and ground them to a powder for preservation. When settlers did arrive, the sauce was immediately adopted and improved upon by mixing whole berries with molasses, adding a piece of preserved lemon peel and boiling. Nowadays, blueberry fanciers can make an excellent sauce in a microwave oven.

RECIPE

Blueberry Sauce

Place 2 cups blueberries, 3 Tbsp sugar and ½ tsp grated lemon peel in a microwavable bowl, cover with vented plastic wrap and zap on high for 3 minutes, stirring once.

BLUEBERRY VINEGAR—a delicious vinegar made either with pure blueberry juice or by soaking the berries in cider vinegar, this latter method being the way most commercial blueberry vinegars are manufactured.

BOILED DRESSING—an iconic Nova Scotia salad dressing used instead of butter or mayonnaise.

RECIPE

Boiled Dressing

Beat 4 eggs in double boiler while slowly adding 6 Tbsp flour and 2 cups hot water. Beat in 1 cup cider vinegar, 6 Tbsp sugar, ¼ cup butter, 4 tsp dry mustard and 2 tsp salt and continue beating until creamy. Kept in a refrigerator, this tasty dressing will stay fresh for weeks.

B

BOILED RAISIN CAKE—a Newfoundland dessert cake that is easy to make and delicious. It smells divine while baking and is always half eaten before dinner time.

> ### RECIPE
>
> *Boiled Raisin Cake*
>
> *Add ½ lb butter, 1 cup sugar, ½ cup molasses, 2 cups raisins and 1 tsp each cinnamon and cloves to 3 cups water. Boil for 15 minutes. Let mixture cool and add 1 beaten egg, 3 cups flour and 2 tsp baking soda; mix well. Pour into greased tube pan and bake at 350° F for 1 hour.*

BOOT HEELS. *See* fat Archies.

BORAGE (*Borago officinalis*; also called bugloss, starflower)— a non-native plant brought along and planted by early French settlers for use as salad greens. It tastes like cucumber and somehow makes a good flavouring for wine  and cider. Now a commercial crop in the Prairie Provinces, seeds from this flowering plant have both medicinal and culinary properties. High in omega-6 fatty acids, oil pressed from seeds goes to supply the health-food trade, while a small percentage of seed is used for culinary purposes and is especially good toasted. Borage flowers are used by upscale chefs to decorate salads and fish dishes, and bees produce a marvellous honey from the pollen.

BOSS RIBS—slang for roast buffalo hump, the most tender meat of the plains bison. In the early years of the 19th century, European hunters killed buffalo for the boss rib and left the carcass to rot.

B

BOUILLABAISSE GASPE—a stew with cod and other fish introduced to the Gaspe area of Quebec by French fishermen and naturalized by the use of local fish.

BOUILLI—a traditional Acadian/Cajun ham and vegetable harvest meal widely adopted by Quebec habitants and modern-day New Orleans restaurants.

BOUILLI CANADIEN. See jiggs dinner.

BOUILLOTTE DE LIEVRE (also called rabbit stew)—an iconic 18th-century habitant dish that mixed rabbit or hare with other game meats, salt pork, onions and flour to thicken. Going west, pioneer settlers had to travel through Quebec, and the habitant rabbit stew recipe went along for the ride; it was a good thing too, because many settlers found rabbit on the menu nearly every night for years.

BOVRIL—a liquid beef extract invented by a Scotsman, John Lawson Johnston, in 1870 and manufactured in England for the British and French armies. Called Johnston's Fluid Beef, the extract was a great success, but in 1879, Johnston's factory burned to the ground. To be nearer a plentiful beef supply, he rebuilt the factory in Montreal. During the winters from 1881 to 1884, Johnston dispensed his hot beef extract drink from the ice palaces constructed at the Montreal Winter Carnival, where it became iconic to the festivities. In 1884, Johnston returned to London and began producing liquid beef for the public; capitalizing on his success in Canada, he would attend expositions and fairs and dispense his hot beverage from miniature ice palaces constructed of glass. At the South Kensington Exposition of 1887, the words "Bovril Brand" first appeared on the chubby glass retail bottles under the embossed "Johnston's Liquid Beef."

B

TRIVIA

Bovril

- The name Bovril is a Johnston-inspired contraction of *bos*, the Latin word for ox, and *vril*, a fictional electric fluid from English author Lord Bulwer-Lytton's then-popular novel, *The Coming Race*.

- John Lawson Johnston passed away at the turn of 20th century, but he done well, as his Bovril Company owned cattle ranches in Argentina and controlled the raising and slaughter of almost 2 million beef cows. However, in 1902, along came a company with an almost identical tasting, but much cheaper product it called Marmite. By 1920, Marmite sales had eclipsed Bovril, and the Bovril Company responded in proper British fashion by buying the Marmite Company. In 1990, the Bovril Company was bought by Best Foods, and in 2000, that company was purchased by the mighty Unilever conglomerate.

- Sometime before the dawn of the 20th century, Bovril switched from a stubby glass bottle to an earthenware crock with a paper label, and in 1924, the company switched to the chubby brown glass bottle recognized around the world.

BOXBERRY. *See* wintergreen.

BRAISED EEL—skinned eel browned in a pan with butter, capers and parsley and then covered and simmered in white wine for 20 to 30 minutes. Eels were an important food item for early settlers. Along with sturgeon, they were fished from the St. Lawrence River near Quebec City, salted and used year-round.

BREAD—the staff of life, made from milled kernels of wheat, corn, rye, barley, oats or almost anything that can be dried and ground to flour. Flour, water, soda or yeast, a spoonful of sugar, a pinch of salt—and voila, bread dough. A 10-minute knead, some time to rise, and into the oven it goes to work its olfactory magic.

B

THE MILLING PROCESS

Newly arrived pioneer cooks made bread from whatever flour they brought along, usually lyed cornmeal. Wheat seed went into the ground after corn and potatoes, followed by barley, peas and oats—all crops that after milling into flour could make bread. Milling would have been a problem for the earliest settlers, who had to rely on a flail and blanket method to thresh grain. Beaten off the stalks, the grain was tossed up and down on a blanket by two people, with one guiding threshed grain onto the floor. To turn threshed grain into flour, settlers used a burned-out tree stump with a milling stone set into the middle. Grain was placed onto the stone, and another stone with a handle was set on top. Crank, crank, take off the stone, brush off a little flour and wipe the brow. It was hard work, usually done by women as they stared out into the forest. They would have noticed that nut trees were everywhere—beechnuts, chestnuts, walnuts, hickory— and in no time at all those women had gathered up the nuts, dried and shelled them, and into the grinder they went. Milled nutmeats used to bulk up expensive wheat flour, produced tasty breads and made some welcome additions to the Canadian food experience.

BREAD PUDDING—sliced bread soaked in egg custard and baked until the little buttered ends get all crispy brown. It's lovely stuff, and very English, but in the early days maple sugar put a "made in Canada" stamp on our pudding.

B

HISTORY OF WHEAT IN CANADA

Canada's contribution to a better staff for the entire planet is so immeasurably steeped in misery and sacrifice that it warrants a worldwide day of remembrance for its pioneers. Wheat arrived on the Canadian prairies in 1812. It was a native English variety brought by the original Scottish settlers to the Selkirk colony at the junction of the Red and Assiniboine rivers. They planted winter and spring wheat, and both crops failed. They planted again the next year, and again, the crops failed—but the fertile land yielded up a good supply of potatoes and turnips.

Undaunted by the two previous failures, the settlers hove to their ploughs and set wheat seed once again, but in spring 1815, they were attacked by Metis rebels and were driven off their land. Rescued by a relief column sent by Lord Selkirk, the settlers returned to find their wheat growing well enough to give them a harvest. The next year, in spring 1816, the Metis attacked again, causing heavy damage. In fall 1817, with the wheat standing tall in the fields, a hurricane struck and levelled everything.

In spring 1818, something completely unexpected descended on the fields like a black cloud—grasshoppers, and so many they consumed the prairie like fire. The farmers were done; the grasshoppers had left them with very little seed for next year's planting, and they moved off their land to hunt buffalo. The next spring, they returned to plant what little seed they had, only to have the grasshoppers return.

In 1820, with no seed, the settlement sent men to the U.S. to purchase bushels of seed, to be barged up the Red River in time for a late spring planting. That fall, the grasshoppers returned—only for a short time, but the crop had been late into the ground and the yield was only enough for next year's seed; the men went back to hunting buffalo.

B

It went like that for another two decades. Even when the weather held, diseases called rust and smut decimated crops.

In 1842, a miracle occurred—not on the prairies but in the tiny settlement of Otonabee, near Peterborough, Canada West (Ontario). The Otonabee farmer's name was David Fife, and the miracle was a packet of Ukrainian wheat called Halychanka scooped from a ship in Glasgow harbour by a friend and sent to David in spring 1842. Not sure if the variety was winter or spring, he popped some seeds into the ground, only to find it was winter wheat and it failed to ripen. Undaunted, he planted the remainder in the fall only to have all but three ears of grain eaten by his cow when it came up the next year. Come spring 1844, he remembered the three saved ears and planted them in a small experimental plot. Those seeds grew well, but most succumbed to the ever-present rust disease before harvest.

Saving the seeds that survived rust, David Fife popped them into the ground and the next fall was rewarded with his miracle: the wheat stalks in his plot grew faster, taller and stronger than any of his normal Siberian wheat variety and showed no signs of rust or smut. He immediately planted his entire crop, and the next fall saw a bumper crop and enough seed to share his good fortune with neighbours, who called their bumper crops of rust-free wheat Red Fife after the grain's red colour and the miracle worker from Otonabee.

BREAD-AND-BUTTER PICKLES—almost every Canadian over the age of 50 can remember having to slice the cukes for these pickles, and hear mom's nagging to "slice 'em thinner."

B

RECIPE

Bread-and-Butter Pickles

Thinly slice 3 quarts washed, unskinned cukes into a large bowl and toss with 3 cups pearl onions and perhaps some finely chopped green and red pepper (optional but good). Pour over a mixture of 8 cups hot water and 1 cup pickling salt. Let stand 3–4 hours. In a large saucepan combine 6 cups white vinegar, 3 cups sugar, 1½ tsp turmeric, 1 tsp mustard seeds and 1 tsp celery seeds, and bring to a boil over medium heat. Add cukes, return to a boil and remove from heat. Ladle into 2-cup Mason jars and boil sealed jars in a water bath for 10 minutes. Will keep in a cool place for up to 1 year.

BREADROOT. See *pomme-de-prairie.*

BRETON CRACKERS—Canada's favourite since 1983, a good-for-you snack made with 12 grains and no artificial ingredients. Baked by Dare Foods, a Kitchener, Ontario, company with more than a century-long history, the crackers are available in supermarkets nationwide.

BREWIS—usually pronounced "broos," a Newfoundland word for the breaking up or "bruising" of hardtack, a ship's biscuit baked by provisioners for long sea voyages. Impervious to water and insects, the rock-hard biscuits required softening before eating. Historically they were set upon the overturned convex lid of a Dutch oven along with a ladle or two of the pot's contents, usually a salt fish stew, from which comes the famous fish 'n' brewis dish. In the past, brewis also meant a dish of softened broken-up biscuits mixed with flaked cod and drizzled with pork fat—yummy. Brewis biscuits are baked by the Purity Company in Newfoundland and sold in the U.S. under the Pilot brand.

BRISLING. *See* Atlantic herring.

BRITCHINS—fried egg sacks, the roe, of codfish; usually fried in cubed salt pork called scrunchions.

BROME LAKE DUCK—a Canadian gastronomic delight since 1912, when Brome Lake Ducks Limited set up shop on the shore of the Eastern Township's Lac Brome. Their goal, to breed the meatiest and finest-tasting duck in the entire world, caught the public's attention, and today the company ships out more than 2 million dressed birds annually. Quack, quack and pass the dewberry sauce.

BROWN SUGAR PIE—of Acadian origin and a precursor to the famed butter tart, this sweet, easy-to-make dessert pie has evolved from a molasses and milk pie to brown sugar and condensed milk and is much better for the transition.

B

RECIPE

Brown Sugar Pie

In a bowl, mix together 1 cup brown sugar, 3 Tbsp flour and ¼ tsp salt, and spread evenly into an unbaked pie shell. Carefully pour over the contents of a 12 oz can of condensed milk, dot with 3 tsp butter and sprinkle on cinnamon. Bake at 350° F for 50–60 minutes or until a knife comes out clean. Let cool, then refrigerate before serving.

BUBBLY BAKE—a favourite Maritime seafood casserole made with fresh scallops, butter, cream, mushrooms, green onions, white wine and a bread crumb topping.

BUCKWHEAT PANCAKES—pioneer breakfast cakes made from a batter of buckwheat flour, water, yeast and a pinch of salt. The batter is set aside to rise for a few hours, then it is puddled into a pan and fried in lard.

B

RECIPE

Buckwheat Pancakes

Beat about 3 pints sifted buckwheat flour, 1 tsp salt and ½ cup good barm (yeast) with enough fresh, warm milk to make a batter. Cover and set aside for the night in a warm place. In the morning, grease up a hot griddle and spoon on batter in puddles until the pan is full, but do not allow the pancakes to touch each other. If your lard or butter is hot enough, the cakes will set as you spoon them on and will cook up as light as feathers. Serve hot with butter and top with maple syrup, apple syrup, molasses or treacle.

BUCKWHEAT

Grown in England to feed hogs and fowl and brought to Canada by the earliest settlers for that purpose, milled buckwheat saw other uses: as a wheat flour extender, stew thickener and, of course...pancakes. Buckwheat grew easily in Canada, and small fields of the crop were common to almost every farm, turning the buckwheat pancake into a breakfast staple. A big stack topped with butter and drizzled with maple syrup put smiles on the faces of pioneer farmers and will do the same for you.

BUDDHA DOGS—a Canadian original from Picton, Ontario, and not just another hotdog. Buddha dogs are made with aged beef and come on a special soft bun and fresh condiments. Buddha is slowly spreading across the nation and will soon be in your town, along with its many variations: poutine Buddha dog, roast turkey Buddha dog and the beans and frank Buddha dog. Oh, and they have a yummy cheese sauce made with aged Pine River cheddar that is to die for.

BUFFALO COD. *See* ling cod.

BUFFALOBERRY JAM (also called bearberry jam, soapberry jam, soopolallie jam)—a favourite of prairie pioneer farmers; made from berries of the buffaloberry shrub (*Shepherdia canadensis*). The tart, red and yellow berries are high in pectin and are easily turned into delicious jams and jellies and some-times wines. On the west coast, First Nations called the berries soopolallies, and by mixing them with sweet berries and beating them frothy could make a sweet dessert reminiscent of ice cream.

B

BUFFALOBERRY POPCORN (also called bearberry pop-corn)—fried in oil, berries of the common buffaloberry (bearberry) will pop like popcorn. The popped kernels are pink and need a lot of butter and salt because they have little taste.

TRIVIA

Buffaloberries

- Buffaloberry shrubs have spiny tips and may grow to 3 metres tall, making harvesting a sometimes-painful experience. Foragers will usually wait for the berries to over-ripen, then shake the berries off the shrub onto catch cloths.
- Pioneers sometimes brewed the berries into a quick wine or beer, as it will completely ferment in 24 hours.

BUGLOSS. *See* borage.

BULL TROUT. *See* Dolly Varden trout.

BUMBLEBERRY PIE—a double-crust pastry pie with a varied berry filling that most often consists of a mixture of raspberries, blueberries, saskatoons and quartered strawberries. It was a prairie favourite but was included in the recipe journals of most Canadian cooks.

B

BURNS CHUCKWAGON DINNER—a canned beef stew so popular in the late 1940s and early 1950s that it sponsored a television show, *Burns Chuckwagon from the Stampede Corral*. Manufactured by Burns Foods, the West's largest beef packer (now controlled by Maple Leaf Foods), the yummy stew in the big can fed countless numbers of camp kids, cottagers and lumber and mine workers. Gone but not forgotten, the stew is memorialized on the menus of many western restaurants as "chuckwagon dinner."

BUTTER BRICKLE ICE CREAM—a popular, bits of toffee ice cream flavour in the U.S. beginning in 1930s. The ice cream became a naturalized, original Canadian flavour in the 1950s when J.B. Jackson Limited, a Simcoe, Ontario, novelty ice cream manufacturer, began using crushed Heath Bars in their formulation.

BUTTER DROP CAKES—recipe #179 from *The Cook Not Mad* (1831) combines 4 eggs, 1 lb each of flour and sugar, ¼ lb butter, a touch of mace and 2 Tbsp rose water; bake in tin pans.

BUTTER TART—a pioneer dessert tart made with easily obtainable ingredients: eggs, butter, corn syrup, brown sugar or molasses, salt and dried currants or raisins. Butter tart popularity has withstood the test of time to become iconic to the Canadian food experience.

BUTTERMILK PIE—an Acadian bottom crust dessert pie with a custard filling of boiled buttermilk, eggs, lemon, sugar, a pinch of salt and cornstarch. The recipe originated to use whey left over from butter making; this delicious pie is still a huge favourite with Maritimers, and recipes are available online.

BUTTERNUT SOUP (also called white walnut soup, oilnut soup)—a delicious soup made by pioneers from nuts of the native butternut tree (*Juglans cinerea*), a member of the Walnut family.

B

RECIPE

Butternut Soup

Add 1 cup crushed butternuts to 2 cups chicken stock, 1 diced onion, 1 chopped celery stalk, 1½ cups milk, 1 tsp salt, 3 Tbsp butter and ¼ tsp black pepper. Cook 10 minutes, then put the mixture through a sieve or give it a few spins in a food processor, and serve piping hot with a dab of butter.

BUTTERNUTS

Butternuts were a boon to pioneers settling in the St. Lawrence and Great Lakes areas. Most forests contained large numbers of butternut trees, which produce a nut that yields almost 60 percent of its weight in oil. Easily gathered from the ground, and such numbers that squirrels got sick of eating them, the nuts were either dried or macerated into cooking oil by a stone grain mill. Unfortunately for the tree and nut lovers, the wood became prized by furniture makers, and later the trees fell victim to an invasive canker disease. A few survive, but not enough to make squirrels sick of eating the nuts, and finding them on the ground these days is nearly impossible.

BUTTERSCOTCH—the pioneer's chocolate, and a confection that has endured the centuries. To make, heat 1 lb brown sugar until melted, then add 4 oz creamed butter and stir until it reaches hardball consistency. Pour onto a greased cookie sheet and score into squares. When cool, break into squares and enjoy.

B

BUTTERSCOTCH PIE—a scrumptious dessert pie made with our pioneer settlers' favourite flavouring.

RECIPE

Butterscotch Pie

Melt 2 Tbsp butter in a saucepan. Stir in ¾ cup brown sugar and continue stirring until thick. In a bowl, combine 2 cups milk, ¼ cup cornstarch and a pinch of salt, and stir. Gradually whisk bowl contents into saucepan and cook for 2–3 minutes until thick. In a small bowl, beat 2 eggs lightly, stir in a little of the hot mixture, add to saucepan and cook while whisking for 2–3 minutes until thick. Remove from heat, stir in 1 tsp vanilla and pour into a pre-baked, 9 inch pie shell. Bake with or without meringue topping for 13–15 minutes at 350° F.

C

CALGARY REDEYE—a mixture of beer and Clamato juice—a purely western thing.

CALIFORNIA ROLL—in spite of the name, this inside-out sushi is our very own, having been invented in the 1970s by Japanese Canadian chef Hidekuzu Tojo, who is also credited with inventing the smoked salmon BC roll.

CALLIBOGUS—spruce beer with rum and molasses added to it. It was an early Newfoundland alcoholic libation whence sprang the slang word "bogus," meaning counterfeit.

CANADA DRY GINGER ALE—the "champagne of ginger ales." It was the brainchild of Toronto chemist John J. McLaughlin, one of Canadian automobile mogul Sam McLaughlin's three sons. In 1890, John McLaughlin opened a seltzer plant in Toronto, and ginger beer seemed a natural progression. But everyone made ginger beer, so he took another path and invented a crisper-tasting product. The brand got a big boost during Prohibition days because it masked the off-flavour of bathtub gin.

CANADA GOOSE CASSEROLE—a favourite of early settlers during spring and fall migrations of the geese. During the 18th and early 19th centuries, the Canada goose (*Branta canadensis*) was almost hunted to extinction, but conservation laws allowed the species to make a comeback. Nowadays the bird is considered more pest than dinner.

CANADA PLUM COMPOTE—a dessert made with boiled fruit in sugar water, and a fall favourite of pioneer families lucky enough to have settled near native Canadian wild plum trees (*Prunus nigra*).

CANADA RICE. *See* wild rice.

CANADA SNAKEROOT. *See* wild ginger.

CANADIAN BACON—it's not a term used in Canada, but in Britain it means bacon from Canada, and to Americans it is a cut of pork loin, or back bacon. *See also* back bacon, peameal bacon.

CANADIAN FONDA. *See* fonda.

CANDLEFISH. *See* eulachon.

CAPE BRETON PORK PIE—not a shred of pork goes into this classic Cape Breton chopped date and molasses dessert tart, but at its inception in the 18th century it may have included pork fat in the pastry.

CAPE GOOSEBERRY. *See* ground cherry.

CAPELIN (*Mallotus villosus*; also called caplin, shishamo)— a close relative of freshwater smelt, this small, silvery fish schools in the arctic and subarctic areas of both the Pacific and Atlantic oceans and comes ashore to spawn every spring. In Newfoundland, the spawn, called a "caplin scull," is a major springtime event, with waves of the little fish rolling onto beaches while residents scoop them up in dip nets or buckets. Salt dried capelin is used as snack food, and the fish are also canned, frozen and shipped to Japan with roe intact for a smoked finger food called shishamo.

CAPILLAIRE (*Chiogenus hispidata*; also called snowberry)— a round, white berry with an acidic but pleasant taste. Widely foraged by Maritimers to make jelly, capillaire were much loved by early trappers, as the berries ripen late and hang onto the branches well into winter.

CAPLIN. *See* capelin.

CARAMILK BAR—an iconic Canadian chocolate bar introduced in the 1960s by the William Nielson Company and now manufactured by Cadbury Adams. Incidentally, the secret to how they get the creamy filling into the bar is an enzyme called invertase, the same enzyme used by honeybees to convert pollen into liquid honey.

CARIBOU (*Rangifer tarandus*)—Canada's most northern communities use this animal to supply us with sustainable wild game meat products that are available at specialty meat shops across the country.

TRIVIA

Caribou

Caribou are plentiful in the Northwest Territories and range over a million square kilometres in herds that may number in the hundreds of thousands. The largest, roaming between Yellowknife and the Arctic and called the Bathurst herd, has at times exceeded a half million animals, but those numbers have diminished over the last decade owing to forest fires that disrupt migration and breeding cycles. Other large herds roaming the north country include the Beverly, Qamanirjuag and Ahiak herds, from which around 20,000 animals are harvested annually.

C

CARIBOU PRIME RIB ROAST—a long-time favourite Sunday dinner roast for northern diners, now enjoyed in other areas of Canada thanks to government initiatives to establish commercial packing facilities in regions of the Far North.

RECIPE

Caribou Prime Rib Roast

Lard the roast, cook for 20 minutes at 450° F, then reduce the temperature to 350° F and cook for 2 hours or until tender.

CARIBOU (the drink)—a potent, head-spinning drink made by combining white grain alcohol with red wine; popular in the Yukon.

CARROT PUDDING—an early Canadian settlers' variation of the very English Christmas plum pudding, but with grated carrots as a bolster for scarce ingredients.

TRIVIA

Carrots

Until World War II, carrots were tough and mostly ignored as a vegetable. British hybridizing experiments to increase the beta-carotene in carrots for better night vision for fighter pilots accomplished that goal, but also produced a more tender, sweeter carrot.

CATSUP, CATCHUP. *See* ketchup.

CARROTS AND CHRISTMAS DINNER

To early settlers with British roots, a Christmas dinner in Canada was a connection to home. Plans were made all year to make it special. A goose or turkey could be managed, either domestic or wild, while the potatoes would be stacked in the root cellar along side the onions and the wonderful carrots that, while still tough as nails, grew faster, larger and sweeter than any remembered from home. Cranberries for the sauce had been gathered, dried and stored in the cupboard awaiting preparation, and though the sweetener might be molasses, nobody was going to complain. The bread for stuffing, baked a few days before, would be waiting—cornbread again, but who cared. The anticipation was almost too much, especially when the children knew their mother had somehow made Christmas pudding.

Pioneer life turned most wives into culinary inventors: a few candied berries, two or three mashed potatoes, a pint of molasses, a few cups of Indian meal and a pile of grated sweet carrots turned into a culinary masterpiece. After dinner, Dad would pour on a bit of brandy and, as Mother turned down the lantern, a lit match would turn her marvellous Christmas creation into a wispy blue volcano eliciting squeals of delight from every child.

CATTAIL-ON-THE-COB—boiled flower heads of the common cattail plant (*Typha latifolia*) or the less common, thin cattail (*Typha augustifolia*). Boil 10 minutes, slather in garlic butter and eat like miniature corncobs. Delicious, nutritious and free for the taking almost everywhere in Canada.

C

CATTAILS AND WILD RICE SOUP—a favourite First Nations soup quickly adopted by pioneer settlers and made from tender shoots of the cattail plant—see online instructions for harvesting.

> **RECIPE**
>
> *Cattails and Wild Rice Soup*
>
> *Boil wild rice until soft, and set aside. In a heavy pan sauté ½ cup green onions or ramps in butter until translucent, then add rice, 2 tsp salt, 4 cups chicken broth and a handful of cattail shoots, and simmer for 20 minutes.*

CAVIAR—processed eggs, or roe, of various fish (sturgeon, salmon or whitefish, with sturgeon eggs being the most prized). Canadian caviar harvested from salmon, whitefish, trout, capelin and farm-raised sturgeon have become an important export product thanks to an almost worldwide embargo of the good stuff from the grossly mismanaged Caspian Sea fisheries.

> **STURGEON**
>
> Once common in Canadian rivers and lakes, sturgeon populations have been decimated through overfishing, habitat loss and poor management. More government intervention is needed to prevent the netting of wild fish for the sole purpose of harvesting caviar, which is a most odious practice.

CHARLEVOIX LAMB—a succulent lamb produced in the Charlevoix area of Quebec and designated under the province's region of origin law, the *indication geographic protégée*, or IGP. Flocks are limited to 500 sheep per farmer and are fed a diet of oats and barley to supplement their grass forage.

C

CHARLOCK (*Brassica kaber*; also called wild mustard)—an unfortunate, bring-along seed of early pioneers that escaped into the wild to become a modern-day super weed subject to constant eradication by farmers. However, before it turned outlaw, it served to provide early settlers a respite from bland foods and earned a spot in the Canadian food experience.

CHEAP CAKE—a simple pioneer cake originally made with a soda rising and whatever of these ingredients were on hand: eggs, butter, flour, milk and a pinch of salt.

CHECKERBERRY. *See* wintergreen.

CHEDDAR CHEESE—a hard cow's milk cheese first made in the town of Cheddar, England, but nationalized by Canadian cheese-making techniques, climate, grass and fodder. Born in Ontario, died in Ontario, as the once-famous quality of modern-day Ontario Cheddar has been slowly compromised by provincial government milk quotas, multinational dairy conglomerates and ambivalent consumers. However, quality Cheddar is still produced in Quebec, where big business rules the fromageries but has somehow spared them the humiliation of a sow's ear, cooperative milk supply.

CHEEMO PEROGIES—a filled dumpling popular across the nation, but especially in our Prairie Provinces. Out on the flatlands, if the perogies are not homemade they are Cheemos, made by Heritage Frozen Foods in Edmonton, Alberta, and available nationwide. *See also* perogies.

CHEESE CURDS—the twisty solid bits recovered from milk coagulated by rennet and drained of whey. Pressed into a mould and aged, cheese curds become Cheddar cheese and may be coloured or left naturally white. The rubbery curds are also sold as a snack food, or they are sent to restaurants for poutine.

C

CHEESE

Early settlers to Canada received their land by various means, including by drawing lots, by outright grants or by squatters' petitions. In those formative years, incentives were needed to attract settlers, one of them being a milk cow to be shared by two settlers. While this gratuity was not offered for long, it did serve to begin a trade in milk cows. By the middle of 18th century, almost every farm enjoyed a daily supply of fresh milk and butter. By the time the 19th century rolled around, the cows had multiplied and a few farmers became dairymen, supplying local villages with milk, cream, butter and farmer's cheese.

Around 1830, Hiram Ranny, an American dairyman from Vermont, moved to Oxford County with five cows. Some 20 years later, he was milking over 100 cows and decided to produce a cheese to promote the business. Ranny got to work and created "The Big Cheese," a 1200-pound monster cheese wheel sent to the London Exhibition in London, England. That event excited both the public and the dairymen, and soon Canada had hundreds of cheese factories, with many situated in Oxford County. In 1893, cheese makers from around Perth, Ontario, pooled their resources to create another promotional cheese, the "Canadian Mite," a 22,000-pound monster Cheddar destined for display at the World Columbian Exposition in Chicago. Loaded onto a railcar, the behemoth cheese wheel had people lining the tracks for a peek. While on display in Chicago, it garnered massive crowds and much publicity after it crashed through the floor of the exhibition hall. Back onto a railcar, the huge Cheddar paraded through towns and villages all the way to Halifax, where, after much ceremony, it was loaded onto a ship for a tour of Britain. Finally, after much hoopla, it was cut up and sold. American cheese makers and food writers are

C

constantly claiming the big cheeses as their own, but too bad, America—those biggies belong to Canada.

Cheese is the only segment of Canada's dairy industry that has seen a rise in consumption; other segments—milk, butter and ice cream—have taken consumption hits owing to home market protectionist policies that enable foreign conglomerate dairy owners to charge high prices while preventing smaller processors from selling their products internationally.

TRIVIA

Cheese

• The province of Ontario's 8500 dairy farmers produce 1.5 billion litres of milk annually, and in Quebec, 10,000 farmers convert over 2 billion litres of milk into cheese annually. That amounts to around 55 percent of Canadian production. Quebec is Canada's "big cheese" and is doing the country proud by winning awards around the world.

• Canada has around 200 cheese makers producing approximately 300 million pounds of cheese annually, with over a third of that production being Cheddar cheese.

CHEESE PUFFETS—a kind of easy-to-make popover popular with Ontario settlers.

RECIPE

Cheese Puffets

Take 3 oz grated Cheddar cheese and mix with 1 egg, ½ cup milk, 1 Tbsp flour and a pinch of salt. Pour into buttered ramekins or muffin tins and bake at 400° F for 8–10 minutes.

C

CHERRY BRANDY PIE—the dessert pioneer wives made while hubby was busy turning their cherry crop into backyard *eau de vie.*

CHERRY COBBLER—a favourite dessert of settlers in the area around the Great Lakes. These settlers brought with them pits of both sweet and sour cherries, but mostly they brought the sours, or Montmorency variety, which are quick growers and not as lofty as the sweet cherry. Fast growing and easier picking meant more pies and cobblers for the family. Nowadays, a new strain of slightly sweeter, dwarf Montmorency is replacing the old, and vast orchards are being established in the Prairie Provinces. Look for the cherries at farmers' markets in the very near future—they will make indescribable cobblers.

RECIPE

Cherry Cobbler

Combine 3 cups pitted sour cherries with ¼ cup granulated sugar and the juice of 1 lemon. Set aside. In a bowl mix 1 cup flour, 1 Tbsp each granulated sugar and baking powder, ¼ tsp nutmeg and a pinch of salt. Cut in ¼ cup cold, cubed butter, pour in ½ cup buttermilk and stir into a moist, sticky dough. Place cherries in an 8 inch square dish and place dough over. Bake at 375° F for 30–35 minutes or until the top is brown and bubbly. Serve hot with whipped or ice cream.

CHERRY WHISKY—a delicious alcoholic libation of early Ontario settlers from around the Great Lakes area, it's a decoction of sour cherries and backyard whisky sweetened with sugar. In other areas of Canada, different fruits were used to soothe the flame of backyard whisky.

C

WHISKY

Many new Canadians brought along seeds for planting, but only a few Scots and Irishmen possessed the necessary skills to ferment mash and distil a decent-tasting whisky to supply general stores. Settlers with little or no skill made backyard whisky that needed fruit and sweetening to make drinkable. Fruit-flavoured whiskies still maintain a modicum of popularity with Canadians, as almost every distiller markets the product in some form: cherry and apricot brandies, peach delight and of course our long-time favourite...cherry whisky.

CHESTNUT (*Castanea dentata*; also called American chestnut)—a once-prominent, edible nut–producing tree of the Carolinian belt of southern Ontario. The nuts, a mainstay food crop for both native peoples and settlers, were sweet and nutritious, and since they flowered in early summer and never suffered frost damage, the harvest was reliable. Mature chestnut trees could produce up to 6000 nuts and became a lumberman's delight, as the wood was easily worked and long lasting. Both nuts and lumber from hundreds of thousands of trees were exported for over a century, but then the blight arrived. By 1945, the trees were but a memory. However, a few proved blight resistant, and today those trees are being propagated for the benefit of future generations.

C

Chestnut Blight

The blight that caused the quick demise of millions of North America's sweet chestnut trees arrived at New York's Bronx Zoo from Japan.

CHESTNUT MEAL—roasted or dried sweet chestnuts ground into flour and used as wheat flour extender and stew thickener or as a main ingredient in cakes, puddings and pie pastries.

CHEVRE. *See* goat cheese.

CHEVRE NOIR CHEESE—hard, goat's milk Cheddar cheese made in Chesterfield, Quebec, by Fromagerie Tournevent.

CHICKEN BONE CANDY—a pink, cinnamon and chocolate, chicken bone–shaped candy made by New Brunswick's Ganong Bros. factory since 1885.

GANONG BROS.

Ganong's company motto says it all—"Canada's Chocolate Family"—and indeed they are. The entire family has been devoted to producing fine chocolates and candy since the company's 1873 inception in St. Stephen, New Brunswick. Canada's oldest candy company currently employs 400 people, distributes across the nation and exports to the U.S. and Britain.

CHICKEN CHOW MEIN—a Canadian Chinese dish different from Americanized versions in that it is usually served on a bed of crispy fried golden noodles.

CHICORY (*Cichorium intybus*)—a member of the Sunflower family of plants, chicory is a much-foraged flavouring for soups and stews, while the dried and roasted roots make an almost-acceptable substitute for coffee. Much used by early settlers, the herb is still popular, widely foraged and available at farmers' markets.

CHICOTAI—a cloudberry liqueur from the Côte Nord area of Quebec.

CHINESE PIE. See *pâté chinois*.

CHITLIN AND PEA—fried male and female codfish reproductive organs, a Newfoundland specialty.

CHOCOLATE ROOT. *See* Indian chocolate.

CHOKECHERRY JAM—a favourite with prairie pioneers, but the jam required long boiling to set up. It's much easier to make today with liquid pectin.

RECIPE

Chokecherry Jam

Boil chokecherries until the skins pop; strain through a jelly bag, squeezing the bag for every last drop of juice. For every 6 cups juice, add 13 cups sugar. Boil 5 minutes, then remove from heat. Add 1 bottle liquid pectin, skim and pour into sterilized bottles.

CHOKECHERRY WINE—an alcoholic, crock-fermented beverage popular with pioneer men and made from abundant, almost inedible chokecherries. To make it, you mash the berries, pour them into a crock, add sugar, water, a few cloves and a shake of cinnamon and let it sit in the sunshine for a few days.

CHOP SUEY—a Canadianized Chinese "hash" of stir-fried meat, poultry or fish cooked with bean sprouts and assorted vegetables. Thought to be invented in either San Francisco or Vancouver,

C

chop suey is actually a culinary variation of *shap sui*, a Chinese stir-fry of offal and mixed vegetables.

CHOW CHOW. *See* green tomato chow chow.

CHRISTIE'S ARROWROOT COOKIES—a mother's favourite snack for toddlers since 1906. You bake good cookies, Mr. Christie, despite being just a cog in the big wheel mega food conglomerate called Kraft.

CHUCKWAGON BREAKFAST—flapjacks and syrup with bacon and coffee; a culinary symbol of western hospitality originating at the 1923 Calgary Stampede and now customary at all rodeos, race events and fairs.

CIPAILLE (also called sea pie)—an iconic French Canadian layered pie made with all turkey, duck, chicken, pigeon, partridge or a combination in separate layers. Historically peculiar to English ships, sea pies baked in large cauldrons were easy to transport, and the protective crust maintained product freshness for weeks. *Cipaille* is still a Quebec favourite and is usually made with chicken.

TRIVIA

Cipaille

- Considered the forerunner of tourtiere, the English sea pie entered Canadian cuisine through a phonetic mix-up at the Gaspe Peninsula; sea pie became *la six pâtés*, or the six layers of the original Canadian tourtiere.

- Fresh and salted pigeons were plentiful, cheap and a prominent ingredient for the entire evolution from sea pie to tourtiere. The word *tourte* is French for both pigeon and the crockery vessel once used to bake both pies.

C

CISCO (*Coregonus artedii*; also called lake herring)—a member of the Whitefish family once commercially fished from all the Great Lakes, but owing to overfishing, the cisco fishery is now confined to Lake Superior. Ciscos are normally smoked and have a taste and texture similar to ocean herring.

CISELETTE—an Acadian sweet and savory dessert sauce made by frying chopped salt pork until crispy, adding molasses and cooking down to a thick sauce. Still popular in parts of Quebec and the Maritimes, ciselette is usually offered on crepes, toast or fresh baked bread.

CLAM CHOWDER—an east coast favourite, thick soup made from clams, diced potatoes and onions in a cream base flavoured with celery salt. While the Americans like to think of chowders as being their own, the word chowder is derived from the French *chaudiére*, meaning "one pot," and is surely of French Canadian/ Maritime origin.

CLAM PIE (also called *pâté aux bucardes*)—an ancient Acadian top crust casserole that is still a favourite with Maritimers, who sometimes add lobster meat during the preparation. In the Maritimes, clam pie suppers are popular with tourists, and those pies come in all manner of variation. Most include onions, some have potatoes, top crusts and biscuit tops, but all are delicious.

CLAMATO JUICE—a spiced and seasoned mixture of tomato and clam juice perfected by the American apple juice conglomerate Duffy-Mott with help from the Calgary inventor of the Bloody Caesar cocktail, Walter Chell.

CLENNEDAK—a children's mispronunciation of the brand name Klondike that became the nickname for a popular wax paper–wrapped molasses candy once sold in Quebec.

CLODHOPPERS—chocolate-covered fudge and graham cracker clusters introduced by the Krave Candy Company in Winnipeg in 1996 and available everywhere.

CLOTTED CREAM—made by every pioneer with a cow, and though not an original participant in the Canadian food experience, every cook should know how to make such a scrumptious dollop.

C

> ## RECIPE
>
> ### Clotted Cream
>
> *Pour 1 quart heavy unpasturized cream into a heavy saucepan and place onto a rack in a roasting pan, adding water up to a level with the cream. Simmer 4 hours, and after cooling carefully, lift the coagulated cream off the whey. Chill clotted cream and serve with almost any dessert.*

CLOUDBERRY. *See* bakeapple.

COADY SAUCE (also called molasses coady)—a 16th-century sweet drizzle sauce for figgy duff, a boiled raisin and breadcrumb pudding popular in Newfoundland.

> ## RECIPE
>
> ### Coady Sauce
>
> *Combine 1 cup molasses with ¼ cup each water and butter, and ¼ Tbsp vinegar. Boil and simmer for 10 minutes while stirring.*

CODFISH À LA MONTREAL—butter-basted codfish baked with peeled potatoes and served with a sprinkling of parsley.

CODFISH BALLS—iconic east coast specialty made by combining cooked and minced codfish with mashed potatoes, beaten eggs and butter. Formed into balls and deep fried like doughnuts, they will have you catching a plane east.

CODFISH HASH—like pea soup, this hash was sometimes called a devil's holiday dish, as it was a ubiquitous dinner item for east coast families. Delicious and still a suppertime favourite.

C

> ### RECIPE
> *Codfish Hash*
>
> *Mix picked codfish with mashed potatoes and cut-up pieces of fried salt pork. Add milk and stir, sprinkle some crispy salt pork on top and perhaps a few dabs of butter, and bake until crispy. Turn onto platter and serve.*

CODFISH TONGUES AND CHEEKS—a true east coast favourite, the fishy face parts were traditionally fried in pork fat and served topped with scrunchions, but nowadays are usually rolled in cornmeal and sautéed in butter.

COFFEE CRISP BAR—a better jolt than chicory, the bar that makes a nice light snack was originated by the Rowntree Company and quickly became a Canadian icon, but lost status when Rowntree was absorbed by the mega conglomerate Nestlé. For reasons unknown, Nestlé changed the bar's package, made it thin, and fiddled with the formula until the Coffee Crisp became just another mass-produced candy bar.

COFFEE SUBSTITUTES—early pioneers had many choices for a substitute java fix: roasted wheat, barley, dandelion roots, chicory, various nuts, etc. In the late 19th and early 20th centuries, roasted and ground soybeans, long used in Europe as a cheap coffee substitute, became popular in Canada, especially during the periods of wartime rationing.

COLD-PRESSED CANOLA OIL (low erucic acid rapeseed oil)—an edible vegetable oil extracted from the tiny seeds of hybridized rape plants by gentle pressing rather than the normal chemical solvent method. Light golden in colour with a fresh nutty flavour, cold-pressed canola is subject to rapid oxidation by air and light and is best purchased organically grown and refrigerated, from a reliable shop. Treat yourself to a national treasure.

COLD-PRESSED FLAX OIL—gently pressed oil from the cracked and flaked seeds of the flax plant (*Linum usitatissimum*), it is your basic linseed oil, but nutritionally one of the best sources of omega-3 fatty acids. Buy it fresh, refrigerated and in dark glass bottles because the oil is prone to oxidation. Use it in smoothies, vinaigrettes and dips, but not for frying.

COLMAN'S MUSTARD—iconic worldwide, but especially loved by Canadians ever since its creation by Jeremiah Colman of Norwich, England, in 1814. Colman's bought out another Canadian favourite in 1903, Keen's dry mustard, in the yellow can. *See also* mustard.

COMBUSE—an Acadian codfish stew that resembles pot roast; the fish is cooked with carrots, onions and potatoes with a bit of salt pork.

CONCORD GRAPES—grapes have been used for pies, jams, jellies and wines since 1534, when French explorer Jacques Cartier stepped ashore in the Gaspe and found forests netted with wild vines festooned with tiny, luscious grapes. Called riverbank or fox grape, the wild vines were quickly crossed with European cultivars to produce a cold-hardy, disease-resistant vine with larger fruit called the Concord grape. The Concord is still the most widely grown grape in the Americas.

CONEY, CONNIE. *See* inconnu.

CORN CHOWDER—your basic Iroquois corn soup with a few added ingredients to suit European pioneer tastes, namely butter, flour, milk, cream and diced potatoes. *Also see* corn soup.

CORN ON THE COB—white, or sweet, corn picked immature before all sugar in the kernels is converted to starch. Fresh cobs are boiled, steamed, roasted or barbecued with or without the

C

husk. There are three types of sweet corn. Su comprises most heritage or heirloom varieties, with kernels that quickly lose sweetness after picking. Se, for sugar enhanced, are varieties with more sugar, and although the sweetness lasts longer, they are still at their best when consumed a few days after picking. Sh2, a shrunken gene type, are genetically modified, super-sweet varieties with an installed gene to prevent the conversion of sugar to starch. There is not much taste and the kernels look shrunken, but ears of Sh2 have the long shelf life demanded by supermarkets.

RECIPE

Corn on the Cob

Bring a large pot of water to a rolling boil, throw in 1 Tbsp sugar and boil stripped ears for 5 minutes. Turn off heat and let ears simmer for another 5 minutes. Remove from water, slather with butter, sprinkle on kosher salt and enjoy. Keep in mind that corn fresh from the field is always best and will need less cooking time.

CORN OYSTER (also called mock oyster, battercake)—an easy-to-make, east coast, fried corn fritter usually served as a fish garnish.

RECIPE

Corn Oysters

Take 1 quart canned or fresh corn and add 3 eggs and 4 crushed crackers. Beat well, season and fry in hot oil.

C

CORN

Corn is a huge crop in Canada, especially in Ontario and Quebec, where around 3.2 million acres are devoted to the golden cobs. It's grain corn mostly, to feed livestock and supply ethanol plants, with sweet corn being a small percentage of total acreage. Sweet corn is your basic dent variety (field corn) with a recessive mutation in the gene that converts sugar to starch, an idiosyncrasy first noticed by First Nations cultivators who isolated the stalks, thus effectively creating the first hybridized sweet corn.

Sweet corn is Canada's largest vegetable crop, with over 50,000 acres under cultivation, and while most is canned or frozen, some fresh is always available for summer feasting. For a treat, if you can find them, try old-style hybrid varieties like Seneca Chief, Golden Bantam and Sugar Dots. Cook them soon as you can, before the sugars begin turning to starch. The new, sugar-enhanced hybrids need not be cooked immediately because their sugar content is almost double that of the old varieties— sweeter, but not as tasty.

CORN PIE—a pioneer version of shepherd's pie. Chopped venison or ground beef is browned in oil, layered into a casserole dish and topped with a layer of sweet corn. Top it all off with a layer of mashed potatoes and bake.

C

TRIVIA

Corn

- Explorers returning to France took along corn seed, but it never amounted to much until the English got hold of it. Then it really took off, and in no time at all, the Indian corn (the English called all grains corn) became so important a crop that it became sole owner of the corn name.

- When the French explorer Samuel de Champlain arrived in Canada in the early 17th century, he found vast plantations of hybridized sweet corn under cultivation by bands of the Iroquois nation. Subsequent explorations by Europeans found even larger sweet corn plantations south of Lake Ontario and along the Mississippi River, with some containing different varieties and colours of sweet corn, including popcorn.

CORN SOUP—iconic pioneer sweet corn soup borrowed from the Iroquois, who used flint corn, yellow corn, white sweet corn or dried corn boiled with venison. Europeans added white onion, flour, butter and salt pork. In modern times, corn soup has become the darling of upscale, imaginative restaurant chefs, and the soup now arrives at tables in dozens of variations.

RECIPE

The Best Ever Corn Soup

Cut the kernels off 4 ears of sweet corn into a bowl and use a spoon to scrape bits and juice from the cobs. In a cooking pot, sauté 1 diced white onion, then add 1 tsp chopped thyme and your corn. Cook for 2 minutes, then add 2 oz white flour and stir into a roux. Incorporate 2 oz dry white wine and slowly add 24 oz chicken stock, the spoon scrapings, 6 oz each heavy cream and cooked wild rice, and 8 oz cooked and diced pork shoulder. Bring to a simmer and serve.

C

CORN SYRUP—Bee Hive, Crown Golden and Lily White brands were the ubiquitous corn syrups of late 19th- and early 20th-century Canada. Crown was the brand of choice in Quebec, on the east coast and in BC, while consumers in the other provinces preferred Bee Hive. Corn syrup mania occurred in the 1950s when the major brands associated themselves through advertising with the Dionne quintuplets, and tons of syrup went into baby formulations.

CORNBREAD—an unleavened corn or Indian meal staple of First Nations, adapted to European tastes by the addition of eggs, sweetener, sour milk and baking soda. In pioneer days, cornbread would have been prepared and baked almost daily, and in later years garnered even more appeal with the addition of baking powder.

RECIPE

Cornbread

Scald 1½ cups whole milk and pour into a mixing bowl. Add ¼ cup sugar, 1 Tbsp salt, ¼ cup shortening, ¾ cup water and 1 cup cornmeal, and stir. Prepare yeast (1 envelope); stir with a fork and let it stand for 10 minutes. Pour into mix and stir. Beat in 6 cups flour, working in the last of it by hand. Turn out dough and knead for 10 minutes. Cover and let rise until doubled in volume. Punch down, cut, shape into loaves and place in greased baking tins sprinkled with cornmeal. Butter tops and let rise until double in volume. Bake in preheated 425° F oven for around 30 minutes. Enjoy.

CORNMEAL. *See* Indian meal.

CORNMEAL MOLASSES BREAD—a Nova Scotia specialty that travelled west with every pioneer settler who tasted a slice.

RECIPE

Cornmeal Molasses Bread

In a large bowl mix 1 cup each hot milk, boiling water and yellow cornmeal with 3 Tbsp butter, ½ cup fancy molasses and 2 tsp salt. In a smaller bowl combine 2 Tbsp dry active yeast, 1 tsp sugar and ½ cup warm water, and let stand 15 minutes until frothy. Add yeast mixture to cornmeal mixture, and slowly beat in 5–6 cups flour until thick. Turn onto floured surface and knead in remaining flour until dough is smooth and elastic. Plop dough into buttered bowl and let rise in place for 2 hours. Punch dough, place into 2 or 3 loaf tins, let rise until doubled in size, and bake at 350° F for 1½–2 hours.

C

COSY EGGS (also called whore's eggs)—Newfoundland words for the green sea urchins that are cut open and the roe consumed with a spoon, like a boiled egg.

COTTAGE BEER—our earliest settlers made homebrew using the Indian meal casks muscled from Quebec City to their new homestead. First, they had to boil a mix of water and wheat bran, along with a handful of hops, until the hops sank to the bottom. Then the hot mix was filtered into a cooling tub and, when lukewarm, a few quarts of molasses were added. Once that dissolved, the mix was poured into the casks along with a few spoonfuls of brewers yeast. With the barrel bunged and working, the thirsty pioneer brewer had only to wait four or five days to slake his thirst.

COTTAGE ROLL—the top ends of pork shoulder, the shoulder butt, or sweet pickled cottage roll when pickled in brine.

COWTAILS—a real cream and butter caramel crafted by Barr's Sweet Revenge Confection Company of Saskatoon. Barr's makes a host of prairie products that may be ordered online.

CPR STRAWBERRIES—early railway workers' slang for the daily ration of stewed prunes served to keep them working regular. In some areas of the West, people still refer to prunes as CPR berries.

CRAB (Dungeness, *Cancer magister*; and red rock, *C. productus*)—of the nearly 100 crab species found in BC coastal waters, the Dungeness and the red rock are the most popular owing to their firm, sweet, nutty tasting flesh.

CRAB BOUCHÉES—a BC variation of *bouchées à la reine*, the famous French puff pastry appetizer, with a Dungeness crab–based filling rather than the French chicken and mushroom.

CRABAPPLE JELLY—one of the bygone days' national condiments made from native crabapples that have been softened in a water bath (apples placed in hot water), sieved, mixed with an equal weight of sugar, laced with a few cloves and a stick of cinnamon, boiled for ½ hour and poured into sterilized jars.

CRABAPPLE PIE—a crusted dessert made with thinly sliced, peeled crabapples sprinkled with sugar, cinnamon and a dredge of flour, dotted with butter and topped with crust.

CRANACHAN—a toasted mixture of oats, fruit, sugar and rum, topped with whipped cream and traditionally served at Maritime Christmas dinners.

CRANBERRY CORNBREAD—a Nova Scotia specialty bread that includes cranberries, boiled or canned pumpkin and chopped walnuts. Use a standard recipe with ½ cup milk, add 1 cup each of cranberries and pumpkin and ½ cup chopped walnuts.

CRANBERRY KETCHUP—an east coast favourite so good you must try it.

RECIPE

Cranberry Ketchup

Peel 1 lb onions and chop fine; add 4 lbs cranberries and 2 cups water, and boil until soft. Sieve mixture. Add 4 cups sugar, 2 cups vinegar and 1 tsp each of ground cloves, cinnamon, allspice, salt and pepper, and boil until thick. Makes 6 pints.

C

CRANBERRY PIE—a deep-dish Maritime crusted pie containing fresh cranberries sweetened with molasses and brown sugar.

CRANBERRY SAUCE—an easy-to-make condiment and a pioneer favourite for game and wild fowl.

RECIPE

Cranberry Sauce

Put 1 cup each sugar and water in a saucepan with 2 cups cranberries and boil for 5 minutes.

CRANBERRY WALNUT SALAD—a pioneer, straight from the land, Sunday dinner salad that remains in vogue even today. In the early days, it was a fall salad, made from fresh-picked cranberries, beechnut oil and possibly foraged greens.

RECIPE

Cranberry Walnut Salad

Mix ⅓ cup each cranberries and dried walnuts with salad greens. Dress with an emulsion of nut oil and lemon juice.

C

TRIVIA

Cranberries

- Originally called bog berry, the cranberry has been part of the great Canadian food experience from its very beginnings in the cuisine of First Nations. The Mi'kmaq harvested cranberries long before John Cabot arrived in 1497, and used them for both food and medicine. A few years after Cabot's visit, French and Basque fishermen began arriving, and trade with the Mi'kmaq began in trinkets and iron pots for furs, along with some medicinal information thrown in gratis. If you want to keep your teeth from falling out, drink the juice of bog berries. The fishermen drank lots, dried cranberries went on their trade list, and they sailed the ocean blue with toothy smiles. Cranberries also became every Maritimer's tonic against the dreaded scurvy while the rest of the nautical world suffered and waited a few centuries for lemons and limes.

- Contrary to popular belief, cranberries do not grow in water. Bogs are only flooded from a nearby source to facilitate harvest.

- Cranberries are white until they ripen, and only ripe berries bounce. Modern processors drop berries onto a steel plate after washing, and only those bouncing over a 10-centimetre-high barrier are allowed to proceed.

- The red in cranberries indicates the presence of anthocyanins, flavonoids with antioxidant, antimicrobial and cholesterol-lowering properties.

CRAYFISH PIE—a favourite of Acadians who took their love of crayfish with them to Louisiana during their forced removal from Nova Scotia. During the initial colonization of Acadia and New France, rivers and streams abounded with crayfish, but by the middle of the 18th century, most were overfished and depleted of crayfish. Down, but not out, crayfish are still enjoyed by many Quebec cottagers who trap the miniature lobsters, keep them in submerged traps for a day to clear their intestines, then boil and eat the tails with drawn butter or seafood sauce. For many years, my parents kept a cottage in the Gatineau Valley, north of Ottawa, and prodigal visits would see me working crayfish traps and boiling up a mess of one-bite delights.

CRAZY CAKE. *See* wacky cake.

CREAM OF WHEAT PUDDING. *See* mush pudding.

CREAMED CODFISH—an east coast favourite supper dish both then and now.

RECIPE

Creamed Codfish

Soak salt cod at least 24 hours and boil until tender in water containing 1 Tbsp vinegar. Remove any bones while hot, let cool and flake the fish. Prepare a roux from 2 Tbsp each butter and flour and 1 cup milk; add 2 beaten eggs. When well mixed, add flaked fish and a squeeze of lemon juice, and cook for 2 minutes while stirring. Serve with a wedge of lemon and a sprinkle of chopped parsley.

CREAMED CORN—a favourite of pioneer families and easy-peasy to make; your dinner guests will think you are a culinary magician.

RECIPE

Creamed Corn

Slice kernels from 3 fresh-cooked ears of corn into a cooking pot. Add 1 cup heavy cream, 2 Tbsp butter, salt and pepper to taste, and cook for 10 minutes.

C

CREAMED CORN SOUP—a popular Depression-era day's starter of canned creamed corn mixed with milk, flour, butter, salt and pepper. A little went a long way and it still does, but nowadays this soup is usually made from fresh corn.

CREAMED SALMON ON TOAST—iconic Depression-era dish made by combining canned salmon, cream of mushroom soup and peas, then heating and serving on toast.

CRETONS (also called gorton)—a spiced onion and pork pâté favoured by Quebec habitants.

CRISPY CRUNCH BAR—a crispy toffee centre covered in milk chocolate and sold in a distinctive red and white package. Once a handmade Canadian candy, the bar has bounced around from one recipe-tweaking conglomerate to another and has become just another mass-produced candy bar.

CROQUIGNOLES—a light and flaky Quebecois egg and butter pastry usually dusted with maple sugar.

CROSBY'S MOLASSES—the national favourite since 1897, the year Lorenzo George Crosby packed in his Yarmouth, Nova Scotia, grocery store and moved to St. John, New Brunswick, to open the Crosby Molasses Company. Crosby traded timber and codfish for Caribbean molasses that arrived in 90-pound barrels called puncheons. Still a family-run business, Crosby's clarifies, grades and packs molasses for both retail and industrial use.

CROWBERRY SAUCE. *See* mossberry sauce.

CRYSTAL BEACH SUGAR WAFFLES—uniquely Canadian waffles that were hugely popular in the late 19th and early 20th centuries. They were made famous by the Crystal Beach Amusement Park in Crystal Beach, Ontario, and are now made by the Crystal Beach Candy Company of Fort Erie, Ontario. They are available at the candy company, local retail outlets and online.

CRYSTAL BEACH IN SUMMER

During the latter part of the 19th century, travel came into vogue in America, and though few could afford a shipboard excursion to Europe, almost everyone could manage the cost of a day trip, especially in summer. Summers without air conditioning or electric fans were insufferably hot, and people near water escaped to local beaches, packing them like sardines. Walking about in a soggy wool swimsuit was not fun, and those day-trippers clamoured for something to get them off the beaches, or at least onto a beach less crowded. Americans living in cities around the Great Lakes—Buffalo, Erie, Toledo, Cleveland and Detroit—cast covetous eyes across Lake Erie, to places God had blessed with great beaches and few people.

Americans are ingenious people, and where there is a will there is a way. So was born the excursion ferry, a day-tripper boat to haul folks across the lake to quiet little places like Crystal Beach, Port Dover and Port Stanley, with shallow water that wouldn't wet the wool swimsuits. It was nice, but wading around and picnics soon got boring, and the time was ripe for ingenious Canadians to rise up and build Ferris wheels and, heaven forbid…promenade cars.

However, pushing your wife or your date around in a buggy also got boring, and that caused other amusement rides to be installed. Over the years, those rides became more daring until, in 1927, Crystal Beach installed the Cyclone, a roller coaster designed to scare the wool swimsuits off everyone who dared ride it. The early 20th century was a hey-day for Lake Erie amusement parks. They all had dance halls with big bands, and they all featured thrill rides, but none bettered Crystal Beach, where as many as 20,000 summer day-trippers would descend on the park daily.

C

CURRANT SAUCE—black, red or white currants cooked down into a sweet, fruity condiment or glaze for meat, fowl and wild game. A favourite of pioneer families, currant sauce is still popular and easily made from commercially raised berries.

RECIPE

Currant Sauce

Mash currants and set aside in a warm place for 4 days. Strain through a jelly bag (avoid squeezing), and mix in 2 lbs sugar for every pint of juice. Heat juice in a double boiler until clear and pour into sterilized Mason jars.

To make a glaze for wild game, add breadcrumbs to sauce along with a few cloves, port wine and a dollop of butter.

CURRY—coriander, cayenne, cardamom seed, turmeric, ginger, mace and saffron are the spice ingredients for curry. In 17th-century India, curry was the culinary choice of officers and employees of the British East India Company, an organization that contributed many settlers to Canada. Those settlers brought family, possessions and a love for curry that became nationalized into the Canadian food experience by the use of game meat. Venison curry, if you have never tried it, is a culinary experience.

D

DAD'S OATMEAL COOKIES—a Canadian oatmeal cookie introduced by the Christie Brown Company at the beginning of the 20th century. Mr. Christie, you bake good cookies. In 1928, his company started baking cookies for Nabisco, and in 2000, for Kraft Foods. Aside from the shrinking size, the cookie remains the best milk and coffee dipper in the country.

DAINTIES—a prairie dweller's name for an assortment of baked goods, such as cookies, date squares and jam tarts.

DALL'S SHEEP BURGER—a trapper's delight, chopped, fried and stuck into a sliced bannock roll. There are around 20,000 Dall's sheep traipsing around BC's Mackenzie Mountain territory, and any Canadian with a spare $7000 to $8000 can shoot one and watch their guide prepare the world's priciest burger.

DAMPER DOGS—scorched balls of dough cooked on stove lids; a Newfoundland specialty and a favourite of children.

DANDELION COFFEE—much used by early settlers, the roasted and ground-up roots of the common dandelion (*Taraxacum officinale*) make a surprisingly good coffee substitute, especially if gathered in the fall and mixed with a small amount of ground coffee. Dandy Blend, an American-made dandelion coffee, is available in some Canadian health food stores and online.

DARE CANDIES—our long-time favourite sweet treats: mints, jubes, jellybeans and now RealFruit gummies, most with natural flavours and all made with the finest ingredients available.

D

DARE FOODS

Dare Foods, a Kitchener, Ontario, mostly family-owned company with factories all over North America, ships quality baked goods and candy products to over 25 countries. Except for Viva Puffs, the products are like ambassadors of good taste. Dare is one of Canada's best-run companies, and except for the tropical oil and cacao-covered Viva Puffs, a cookie dumped on them through acquisition, they mostly eschew artificial flavours, harmful chemicals and peanuts. However, Dare's designation as a family-run business has been somewhat compromised by a partial merger with the Canadian dairy conglomerate Saputo.

DARE COOKIES—real chocolate Whippets, Grissol Melba Toast, Ruffles, Normandie Fingers, cream-filled cookies with natural flavours, and many more, including the much-anticipated Girl Guide cookies.

DARK TICKLE CHOCOLATES—all the tastes of Newfoundland and Labrador covered in rich, dark or milk chocolate. A "tickle" is a narrow channel of water, and in Griquet, where the Dark Tickle Company is located, the tickle is shadowed by hills. Cranberry-covered chocolates, bakeapple, blueberry and partridgeberry ganache-centred chocolates, as well as screech rum, jam, jellies, juices, teas, pickles and other east coast delights are all lovingly prepared by traditional methods and are available online.

DATE SQUARES. *See* matrimonial cake.

DEVIL'S FOOD CAKE—a red-coloured chocolate cake, a culinary oddity caused by baking powder turning cocoa red during baking. It is a shared culinary invention, since baking powder was introduced into the U.S. and Canada at about the same time.

DEWBERRIES AND DUCK—dewberries (*Rubus flagellaris*) make a fine sauce for wild or domestic duck. A favourite of pioneer families, the sauce is made by adding ½ cup mashed berries to the juices from the roasting pan along with 3 Tbsp brown sugar and a sprig of rosemary.

DIGBY CHICKEN—an east coast pet name for salt herring, so called because the fish once served as Christmas dinner for impoverished pioneer families.

DIGBY FRIED SCALLOPS—the absolute best way to enjoy the succulent harvest of Digby, Nova Scotia's scallop fishing fleet, the world's largest.

DILLY BEANS—pickled green beans, made popular across Canada after the invention of the Mason jar. Carrots may also be dilled.

DO DOWNS—preserves.

DOLLY VARDEN TROUT (*Salvelinus confluentus*; also called bull trout)—not a trout, but a distant relative and actually a char native to BC and parts of Alberta. An excellent game and eating fish, the Dolly Varden has unfortunately become rare and is a catch and release fish in many areas. It is the provincial fish of Alberta. The bright colours of the fish earned it the name Dolly Varden, after the fashion of dress worn by characters in Charles Dickens' historical novel *Barnaby Rudge*.

DORE. *See* walleye.

DOUGH GODS (also called elephant ears, beaver tails)—bread dough, flattened, fried and drizzled with maple syrup or honey.

DRIED APPLE PIE—a favourite with early pioneer settlers because drying apples was a major preserving method.

> ### RECIPE
>
> #### Dried Apple Pie
>
> *Stew dried apples until tender, then add sugar, cinnamon and a dash of lemon juice. Pour into pie shell, top with pastry and bake for 10–15 minutes.*

DRIED PEAS—whole green and yellow, split green and yellow, and chickpeas, lentils and beans are called pulse crops, and except for the chickpeas, we grow more of them than any other country. It is only fitting since they arrived here with the very earliest pioneers and became a national crop long before wheat became popular. Nowadays, most pulse crops are grown in our Prairie Provinces, especially in Saskatchewan, and exported worldwide.

DUCK AND WILD RICE DINNER—a favourite on the prairies, where the combination of duck and wild rice was readily available: where the wild rice grows, there are ducks.

DUCK FOIE GRÂS—produced by a number farmers across the nation, with the most notable being Aux Champs d'Elise, a 1988 Quebec initiative by Marieville dairy farmers Elise and Annette Francois, who now supply chefs across Canada, Japan and Europe.

DULSE—an edible seaweed (*Palmaria palmata*) harvested from the northern waters of both the Pacific and Atlantic oceans, with the most prized coming from the Bay of Fundy, especially from around the Dark Harbour area of Grand Manan Island.

DUNGENESS CRAB. *See* crab.

DUTCH MESS (also called hugger-in-buff)—a Lunenburg, Nova Scotia, specialty of boiled salt cod and potatoes often topped with onions fried in pork fat.

D

E

EAGLE BRAND SWEETENED CONDENSED MILK—a mix of milk and cane sugar that is vacuum evaporated. Invented by an American, Gail Borden, in 1856 and on the market as Eagle Brand in 1857, the product was first manufactured in Canada at the Ingersoll Dairy in 1899. The sweetened milk had a long shelf life and was great for baking, for whitening coffee and tea, for feeding kids and for military rations, and it could easily be shipped by rail across Canada. Now owned by Smuckers, Eagle Brand is still a fine product and remains our favourite.

EAST COAST PRAWNS. *See* prawns.

ECONOMY CAKE (also called poor-man's cake, poverty cake)—a popular ingredient-saving cake of World War I with no milk, no eggs and no butter. Economy cake became popular again during Depression days and during World War II rationing.

RECIPE

Economy Cake

In a saucepan mix 1 cup each water and brown sugar, 1½ Tbsp each lard and cinnamon, and a pinch of salt, and bring to a boil. Reduce heat, add ½ lb raisins or dried berries and simmer for 15 minutes. Sift 1½ cups flour with ½ tsp baking powder and stir into cooled wet mix. Pour into a greased 9 inch pan and bake at 350° F for 20–30 minutes.

EEL PIE—a casserole topped with pastry. It was a common dish of early settlers along the St. Lawrence River because the slippery, snaky fish could be caught there almost anywhere and at any time of year.

E

TRIVIA

Eel

Eel prepared in any manner was familiar food to our pioneer ancestors. The fish was plentiful in European waters and was served as "food for the masses" but was also a favourite of landed gentry. Modern times have seen a marked decrease in the popularity of eel, probably owing to both the fish's resemblance to snakes and the fatty content of the meat. Up to 60 percent of eel meat is fat, and a good percentage is artery-clogging, saturated fat. Still, a little is not going to hurt, and if you get a chance for a little, make it smoked. Mmmm, good.

EGG CREAM SANDWICH—an Ontario specialty, chopped hard-boiled eggs mixed with cottage cheese, mayonnaise, chopped pimento and seasoning.

EGG FOO YONG—a fried egg, meat and vegetable omelet dish created by Chinese cooks working on 19th-century North American railway expansion.

TRIVIA

Chinese Railway Cooks

Chinese railway cooks created a unique stir-fry cuisine that leaned toward meat rather than traditional Chinese vegetable dishes. Chow mein, chop suey and breaded chicken balls are a few examples of that enduring cuisine.

E

Eggs

Poultry eggs are graded A, B and C, with the A quality reserved for retail. In Canada, eggs are weighed individually and packaged according to weight:

Pewee	less than 42 g
Small	42–48 g
Medium	40–55 g
Large	56–62 g
Extra-large	63–69 g
Jumbo	70 g or more

EGGS IN ASHES—fresh eggs holed with a pin and set into the hot ashes of a hearth. Eggs are cooked and ready to serve when a drop of white appears through the pinprick on top. It was a handy trick in pioneer days and still a good one for modern-day campers.

EISWEIN. *See* ice wine.

ELDERBERRY PANCAKES—a rare treat in early spring when the elderberry tree (*Sambucus canadensis*) blooms. The blossoms are picked, the veins and stems removed and the flowers mixed into buttermilk pancake batter that is quickly popped onto a griddle and fried before the blossoms wilt. Elderberry blossoms impart a delicious nutty flavour to pancakes, which are especially good with butter and high-quality maple syrup.

ELDERBERRY PIE—a delectable dessert pie made from the blue-black fruit of the American elder tree, a species ubiquitous in southern Ontario and Quebec and favourite dessert of pioneer families. Nowadays, this delight is made even better when served with a big scoop of vanilla ice cream.

> **TRIVIA**
>
> **Elderberries**
>
> • Long known to have medicinal qualities, especially for arthritis, the tiny, blue-black berries have been identified as antioxidant rich and cancer fighting and are now a hot property with foragers.
>
> • Elderberries are one of the flavouring components of the popular Italian liqueur Sambuca.

ELDERBERRY WINE—a pioneer favourite because the small, blue-black berries form in clumps and are easily gathered, and both fruit and flowers make a delicious wine.

> **RECIPE**
>
> *Elderberry Wine*
>
> *Soften mashed berries in a covered pan or crock, immerse container in water and turn up the heat. At the simmer, remove berries, sieve and add 1 lb sugar for every 4 cups, along with 8 cups water. Boil the liquid while skimming until scum ceases to rise. Cool, add 2 cups brandy and filter into casks. Set the bung loosely until fermentation stops. Bung tightly and allow 6 months for maturing before clarifying with egg whites.*

ELEPHANT EARS. *See* dough gods.

E

ELK BURGERS—a favourite of early pioneers and trappers; elk meat chopped, fried and stuck into a sliced bannock roll. There is no commercial hunting of elk, but your chances of digging into an elk burger will improve in BC and the Prairie Provinces—that is where around 80,000 of the giant deer roam, with around 5000 taken annually by hunters.

EMPIRE CHEESE—a dairy farmers' cooperative in Campbellford, Ontario, producing a wide range of cheeses with emphasis on aged cow's milk Cheddar. Empire has been crafting cheese since the 1870s and is a consistent winner at both the British Empire Cheese Competition and the Royal Agricultural Winter Fair.

ENGLISH MILK PUNCH—a favourite east coast drink of lemons, rum, milk and nutmeg. The mixture was set aside overnight, filtered through a jelly bag and drunk clear and chilled.

EPERLANS. See fried smelts.

ESKIMO PIE—an ice cream bar on a stick dipped in chocolate and introduced to Canadians in the summer of 1921 by the William Nielson Company, now a division of Kraft Foods.

ESKIMO POTATO. *See* northern rice-root.

EULACHON (*Thaleichthys pacificus*; also called oolichan, candlefish)—an oily member of the Smelt family and an important food source for First Nations of the Pacific coast. Eulachon are the first fish to make a spawning run into BC rivers, and their arrival was, and still is, awaited patiently by native fishermen, flocks of gulls and hundreds of bald eagles.

E

TRIVIA

Eulachon

- In the early days, oil rendered from eulachon enjoyed such an intertribal trade that trails used to transport the oil became the narrow roads called "grease trails" by explorers and pioneer settlers.

- Eulachon contain so much oil that, once dried, an inserted wick will light up the fish like a candle—hence the common name, candlefish.

EVENING PRIMROSE (*Oenothera biennis*; also called fever plant, large rampion)—a biennial native plant with large, hard roots consumed by First Nations. Exported to Europe during the 17th century by the Hudson's Bay Company, the plant is still extensively cultivated there, but for its medicinal oil. Evening primrose roots must be boiled to remove the sharp, peppery taste and then seasoned and doused with butter, or served up fried.

F

FABA BEAN. *See* horse bean.

FALSE SAMPHIRE. *See* goose tongues.

FAMINE FOODS—many native shrubs produce nutritious berries not normally consumed owing to bitter or astringent qualities, while the inner bark of several tree species makes for a palatable soup. Animals not normally seen on tables would appear during hard times: skunk, raccoon, ground hog, porcupine and birds such as robins and blackbirds. *Tripe de roche* (literal translation: rock guts) is an easily found lichen and provides sustenance for the truly desperate. Purslane, or portulaca, is a weed well known to Canadian gardeners, but it can make a passable salad green and was at various times cultivated as a garden crop.

FAT ARCHIES (also called long Johns, boot heels)—a Nova Scotia favourite ginger cookie made thin and crisp, thick and soft, or cut in squares from a sheet. Ginger, used by fishermen to allay the effects of seasickness, was ubiquitous in the Maritimes, and cookies are the preferred way of taking your medicine.

FAT HEN. *See* lamb's quarters.

FEVER PLANT. *See* evening primrose.

FÈVES AU LARD (also called *les binnes*)—baked navy beans cooked with salt pork and sweetened with maple syrup or sugar. A Quebec favourite anytime, but prepared religiously at annual sugaring-off feasts and the many Quebec syrup-gathering operations open to tourists.

FIDDLEHEAD CHOWDER—an east coast spring favourite made as for normal chowder, but substituting fiddleheads for clams or fish.

FIDDLEHEADS—the coiled, unfurled and tender shoots of the ostrich fern (*Matteuccia struthiopteris*). Both foraged and commercially cultivated in New Brunswick and Quebec, fresh fiddleheads are available nationally during early spring and in the frozen section of supermarkets year-round. Jiggle them in a brown paper bag to remove the brown bits, then steam; serve buttered.

F

FIFTH TOWN ARTISANAL CHEESES—goat and sheep's milk cheeses lovingly crafted in Picton, Ontario, at their brand new, world's most ecofriendly dairy. Fifth Town won first prize for goat cheese at the 2009 British Empire Cheese Competition, but their goat/sheep's milk cheese should soon be in the winner's circle at all cheese competitions. Sold only in Ontario for the time being, their cheeses are available online.

FIGGY DUFF—a Newfoundland steamed pudding made from flour or breadcrumbs, molasses, raisins and spices placed into a muslin pudding bag for a few hours of steaming. Newfoundland figgy duff was, and still is, usually served with coady sauce.

TRIVIA

Figgy Duff

- Figgy was a word used by English gentry as a mockery of the fruit used by common folk who could never afford figs: raisins.
- In Newfoundland, all pudding desserts are duffs, a word taken from the English pudding plum duff, and raisins are the figgy.

FILBERTS. *See* hazelnuts.

FIREWEED (*Epilobium* spp.)—a common perennial in Canada's north; the new shoots taste like asparagus when boiled, while the leaves of mature plants make excellent salad greens with a taste reminiscent of spinach.

F

FISH 'N' BREWIS—a traditional Newfoundland and Labrador Sunday morning breakfast dish. Fresh or salt cod was cooked and served with water-softened hardtack biscuits, and usually topped with fried bacon bits called scrunchions. *See also* brewis.

FISH LOAF—a ubiquitous loaf pan dish consisting of flaked fish (cod, haddock, etc.) combined with bread crumbs, chopped celery, onions, green pepper and pimentos, held together by egg, milk, salt, pepper and lemon juice. Cod is best, but during trying times, like economic depressions or wars, canned salmon or tuna will do nicely. Refrigerated overnight, any leftover will slice easily for sandwiches.

FISH STICKS—an easy-to-prepare "fast food" invented in the early 1950s by Newfoundland native Dr. William Forsey Hampton, director of research at General Seafoods.

FIVE ROSES FLOUR—not bleached or blended and milled from only the finest quality wheat, Five Roses flour made Lake of the Woods Milling Company the largest milling concern in the British Commonwealth. From 1887 to 1967, Five Roses flour shipped worldwide and earned both the company and Canada a reputation as the world's premier supplier of wheat and wheat products. Now owned by the U.S. food conglomerate Smuckers, the flour is still one of the best and popular with Canadian cooks.

FIVE ROSES

Lake of the Woods Milling Company published the *Five Roses Cookbook* in 1913. Over the years this cookbook succeeded in upgrading the culinary skills of untold thousands of Canadian housewives and produced a Canadian style of cooking. In 1954, Lake of the Woods Milling was acquired by Ogilvie Flour Mills of Winnipeg, and in 1993, Ogilvie was acquired by the U.S. conglomerate Archer Daniels Midland Company, which a decade or so later sold Canada's favourite flour brand, Five Roses, to Smuckers, the jam people.

F

TRIVIA

Types of Wheat Flour

all-purpose: a bleached or unbleached mix of hard and soft wheat flours with a gluten content of 9–11 percent

bread: bleached or unbleached flour made from hard, red winter wheat with a gluten content of 12.5–14 percent

cake: bleached soft flour with a gluten content around 8 percent

pastry: a commercial grade flour with a gluten content around 9 percent

self-rising: a mixture of all-purpose flour, salt and baking powder

white wheat: unbleached white flour with bran and germ removed at milling

whole wheat: unbleached flour with bran and germ left intact during milling

graham: unbleached whole grain flour with germ and bran removed and bran added back

semolina: course ground durum wheat sifted to remove the fine flour

FLAN AU BLÉ D'INDE—a cornmeal pancake popular in New Brunswick and called johnny cakes in the U.S.

FLAPPER PIE—a graham crusted, custard-filled pie and long-time Prairie favourite.

FLAX SEEDS (*Linum usitatissimum*)—an excellent source of omega-3 and omega-6 fatty acids, flax seeds also contain anti-oxidants with powerful cancer-fighting properties called lignans, and as a bonus, the seeds will keep you regular like nothing else on the planet. Flax seeds are hard as nails and must be milled into a flour for baking bread, but for everything else—smoothies, topping breakfast cereal, etc.—the roasted seeds are best because they develop a rich, buttery flavour. To order online, go to Golden Roasted Flax Seeds.

F

TRIVIA

Flax

• Flax has been growing in Canada since Louis Hébert, Canada's first permanent settler, brought the seeds in 1617, but it never became an important crop until immigrant farmers took flax seeds west in the early 1800s. Now Saskatchewan and Manitoba account for almost half the world's flax production. Nearly all western-grown flax is destined for export as meal, oil and fibre, with a only a tiny amount used by domestic food producers. However, studies have revealed the many healthy attributes to flax, and beginning in 1990, flax has seen a huge increase in demand.

• Linseed oil, a product of flax, is a main constituent of paint and the floor covering linoleum.

• Flax fibres are used in the manufacture of linen cloth, rope and matting.

FLOP. *See* lobcouce.

FLUMMY DUMM—a quick bread made by hunters and fur trappers: combine two handfuls of Indian meal (cornmeal), a little soda, salt and water enough to make a dough, knead a bit, spear onto a stick and hold over a fire until baked.

FOIE GRÂS—enlarged goose livers, an exotic comestible produced in France by force feeding corn to geese. Never a popular food item with Canadians, this gourmet delight has recently gained popularity as duck foie grâs. *See also* duck foie grâs.

F

TRIVIA

Foie Grâs

Animal rights groups around the world have been fighting to have foie grâs banned owing to the force feeding nature of its production. Several countries and states have been persuaded to comply, including California, which has instituted a complete ban of the importation, production or sale of foie grâs from any source.

FONDA (also called Canadian fonda)—a baked egg omelet consisting of a little flour paste stirred into 1 cup milk, 6 eggs separated and beaten lightly, a spoonful of butter and a dash of salt, and mixed together only slightly. Bake for 15 minutes; sprinkle with cinnamon and sugar before serving.

FORESTRY PUDDING—a Canadian settlers' variation of the very English steamed caramel pudding using lard and baking powder to replace eggs and butter, with the cake smothered in butterscotch sauce rather than caramel.

F

FORFAR DAIRY CHEESE—in Portland, Ontario, since 1863, Forfar Dairy produces superlative aged Cheddars using a heat process rather than pasteurization and presses curds the old-fashioned way, in wheels. Forfar makes a wide variety of cheeses including chevre, and all are available at outlets across Canada and online. Cut from a 90-pound wheel, their five-year-old Cheddar is a memorable experience.

FOXBERRY. *See* partridgeberry.

FOXBERRY WINE. *See* squashberry wine.

FRAGRANT SUMAC TEA. *See* sumac tea.

FRANKUM—a Newfoundland word for the resinous sap of spruce trees that is gathered, aged a few days, and used for chewing gum.

FRENCH BREAD—the national loaf of France. Until 1921, when Cousin's Charcutier began baking the bread in Montreal, it was never a product of Canadian bakeries. Nowadays, many artisanal bakers produce French bread, but you have to pick and choose from those to secure a decent loaf. Fat and dusted with flour does not always equate to a real French bread. French bread requires much of a baker: the right flour and yeast, no additives in that flour, hand kneading and long resting times for the dough. Canadians seem to prefer their bread white, sliced, able to last weeks without mould, and on shelves at local supermarkets, or what Newfoundlanders call baker's fog.

FRENCH CANADIAN PEA SOUP. *See* pea soup.

FRENCH TOAST. See *pain perdu.*

FRICÔT—an Acadian word for a meat, fish or poultry stew, as in *Fricôt à la poule*, or chicken stew. Except for fish, both game meats and poultry would be stewed for long periods to tenderize the meats. Nowadays, *fricôt* is still immensely popular in Quebec and parts of the Maritimes, but cooking times are considerably shortened owing to the availability of tender meats and poultry.

FRIED PIG EARS. See *oreilles de crisse.*

FRIED SMELTS (*Osmeridea*; also called *eperlans*)—a family of small fish found in coastal seas, rivers and lakes. Delicious any way you cook them, but especially tasty when purchased from small stands and chip wagons that dot the roadsides along the St. Lawrence River.

FRIED WALLEYE. See walleye.

FRIED-OUT PORK—a Maritime method of cooking salt pork to a crisp for a breakfast meat or scrunchions.

FROG LEGS—the fried or sautéed back legs of the North American bullfrog (*Rana catesbeiana*). This amphibian is doomed to probable extirpation owing to voracious global demand, with France alone importing over 400 million frogs annually. Commercial harvesting in Canada, once a booming enterprise in Ontario, Quebec, New Brunswick and Nova Scotia, has waned and is prohibited in some provincial areas. Introduced into BC as a commercial endeavour, the bullfrog has become a pest and is subject to eradication programs.

FROMAGERIE PERRON CHEESE—family run since 1890, this modern cheese plant in Saint-Prime, Quebec, produces outstanding cheese with emphasis on Cheddar and some raw milk cheddar. Fromagerie Perron is a consistent winner at the Royal Winter Fair, and products are available in Quebec and some Ontario, western and Maritime outlets. For a taste sensation, try their 115th-anniversary raw milk Cheddar, and then write your MP and ask why unpasteurized milk is not made available to cheese makers across the nation.

FROZEN BABY FOOD—another "why didn't I think of that?" product, and a Canadian original made by Mother Hen Baby Food Inc., a Montreal producer of home-style, frozen baby foods.

FRUIT BUTTERS—plums, peaches, berries, apples, etc., mixed with sugar and spices and simmered into a thick, delicious jam spread. Apple and plum butters were popular in our nation's formative years as they made a fair replacement for butter. Nowadays, whizzing the softened fruit in a food processor can reduce the long simmering time.

F

FRUIT COMPOTES—rhubarb rhizomes and peach pits were brought by 18th-century settlers for the express purpose of making compote, a simple dessert of fresh fruits, sugar and spices. There are dozens of recipes, with many found online.

FRUIT LEATHERS—an age-old specialty of First Nations and a kind of byproduct of pemmican production, wherein a portion of pounded berries destined for pemmican was set onto fireside rocks and dried to the consistency of leather.

FRY BREAD—an Ojibwa version of bannock fried in lard. Originally an unleavened cake made with cornmeal, salt and water, fry bread has evolved to include wheat flour and baking soda rising and has become a favourite of western First Nations and many fast-food outlets in those areas.

FUDGE—a "what to do with the kids on a Sunday afternoon?" international culinary treat that became a naturalized Canadian treat through the addition of maple sugar. Maple fudge with all-natural ingredients is a candy extraordinaire.

FUDGE BAR—our version of an American creation and the absolute favourite ice cream novelty bar of the 1960s era. Perfected by J.B. Jackson Limited, a Simcoe, Ontario, ice cream manufacturer, the creamiest, fudgiest bar in the known universe disappeared in the early 1970s when that company became an acquisition of the mega conglomerate Unilever.

FUNGY (also called blueberry grunt)—a deep-dish blueberry pie from Nova Scotia and named fungy for the way steam from juices poked holes in the top pastry, or grunt for the sound steam made while escaping said pastry.

FUSSELL'S THICK CREAM—a canned sterilized milk and long-time Newfoundland favourite. You had to shake the can to make it thick, and now Newfoundlanders can shake tins of Nestlé Carnation Light Condensed Milk, as the Swiss mega conglomerate now owns the Fussell brand and uses the same formulation.

F

G

GALETTE—in France a buckwheat crepe, in French Canadian homes a sugar cookie, and on Quebecois restaurant menus a wheat flour pastry disc usually filled with fresh fruit, folded over and baked like a fruit pasty.

GALVAUDE—a fries and gravy poutine with chunks of turkey or chicken and green peas instead of cheese curds.

GANDY—a Newfoundland pancake fried in pork fat and drizzled with molasses.

GASPEREAU. *See* alewife.

GEAI BLEU CHEESE—a raw cow's milk blue cheese crafted at La Bergerie Aux 4 Vents in Champ Dore, New Brunswick. Supply is limited, but it is available across Canada in larger centres—search online for those centres.

GEODUCK (*Panopea abrupta*; pronounced gooee-duck)—a very large and tasty clam found in the saltwater tidelands of British Columbia's coastal areas. Geoducks are long-lived bivalves, which enable some to attain a considerable size, up to 7 kilograms. Sadly, their numbers have dwindled owing to over-fishing, and in most coastal areas of BC the geoduck clam is a protected species. The geoduck has an Atlantic cousin, the propeller clam (*Cyrtodaria siliqua*), which is not endangered and is a good substitute.

GHOW—a west coast First Nations word meaning tiny herring eggs, or spawn attached to kelp fronds, but to financially hard pressed BC fishermen, the word means another source of income.

GHOW

Called *komochi konbu* in Japan, the ghow, or herring roe on kelp, is a delicacy and much in demand for sushi. Good for the fisherman, good for the herring, because when BC fishermen capture millions of herring to harvest their roe, the herring are unharmed and released back to the sea. Schools of herring are captured by nets and towed to a bay or inlet that has been hand strung with kelp, and after the herring have attached their spawn to the hanging kelp, nets are lifted and the fish are free to leave. It is a sustainable fishery, and Canada accounts for 80 percent of the annual global harvest of 400 to 500 tons.

G

GINGER BEEF—invented in Calgary by George Wong, owner of the Silver Inn Chinese restaurant and originally called Deep Fried Shredded Beef in Chili Sauce, the dish has become a menu fixture of Chinese restaurants nationwide.

GINGER SPICE CAKE—a moist, butter-rich molasses and ginger cake made with either wheat flour or Indian meal. If early settlers had a cow for the butter, they were set. The molasses and spices to make this cake were kitchen staples thanks to constant trade with Caribbean countries. The delicious cake is enjoyed even today, but nowadays, sugar is more commonly employed as sweetener.

GINGERBREAD—a molasses, flour and ginger cake made uniquely Canadian by the substitution of maple sugar for molasses.

G

> **RECIPE**
>
> *Old-fashioned Canadian Gingerbread*
>
> *Sift together 1¾ cup plus 2 Tbsp flour, ½ tsp each baking soda and ground cinnamon, ¼ tsp each ground cloves and ginger, and a pinch of salt. In a mixing bowl, combine 6 Tbsp butter with ⅓ cup maple sugar or cane sugar, and beat until light and fluffy. Add 1 large egg and beat while slowly pouring in ¼ cup dark molasses. Add half the dry ingredients and mix well, then add the other half and slowly incorporate ¼ cup cold water. Pour batter into an 8 x 8 inch pan and bake at 350° F for 30–40 minutes or until a knife inserted into the centre comes out clean. Serve with whipped cream sweetened with maple sugar or syrup.*

GINGERSNAPS—crisp ginger and molasses cookies favoured by east coast fishermen to allay the effects of seasickness.

GLASSWORT. *See* goose tongues.

GOAT CHEESE (also called chevre)—some of the world's finest chevre comes from the Woolwich Dairy in Orangeville, Ontario, and the Mornington Heritage Cheese and Dairy Co-op in Millbank, Ontario, two companies that turn milk from hundreds of Ontario goat farms into snowy white, award-winning goodness. However, smaller artisanal chevre producers abound in Canada: Mariposa Dairy in Oakwood, Ontario, produces a superlative single-herd chevre; Ran-Cher Acres in Aylesford, Nova Scotia, crafts a delightful chevre with a dusting of ash; and also Forfar Dairy near Kingston, Ontario, Hilary's Fine Cheeses in Cobble Hill, BC, Happy Days in Salmon Arm, BC, and Fairwinds Farms in Leduc, Alberta. These are just a few; dozens more are all making the nation proud.

GOLDEN ROASTED FLAX SEEDS—a roasted, buttery, hulled seed product of CanMar Grain Products Ltd. in Regina, Saskatchewan, and a Canadian original. Available in retail and health food outlets as roasted seeds or milled seeds, plain or milled with blueberries, apple cinnamon, pomegranate or chocolate, the seeds can be used in a hundred different health-benefiting ways. Flax seeds are an excellent source of omega-3 and omega-6 fatty acids and contain significant amounts of lignan, an antioxidant with powerful cancer-fighting properties.

G

GOOSE TONGUES—not the tongues of geese, but actually glasswort (*Salicornia europaea*; also called false samphire, pickle weed, sandfire greens). Called goose tongues for the plant shoots' resemblance to those French delights, the shoots have a salty taste of the sea, were a common ingredient in Acadian salads and are still available in farmers' markets. They are commonly used as a nesting salad for fried cod tongues and cheeks.

GOOSEBERRY CRUNCH—a favourite pioneer summer dessert made with plump, fresh gooseberries (*Ribes* spp.), brown sugar and oatmeal.

RECIPE

Gooseberry Crunch

In a bowl, mix until crumbly 1 cup each flour and brown sugar, ¾ cup rolled oats, ½ cup softened butter and 1 tsp cinnamon. Press half of the crumb mixture into a 9 inch buttered pan. In a saucepan combine 1 cup each water and sugar, 2 Tbsp cornstarch and 1 tsp vanilla. Bring to a boil, add 4 cups fresh gooseberries and cool until thick. Pour over pressed crumb, top with remaining crumb and bake at 350° F for 45 minutes. When cooled, cut into squares and serve with whipped cream, maple syrup, ice cream or all three.

GOOSEFOOT. *See* lamb's quarters.

GORTON. *See* cretons.

GOURGANE (*Vicia faba*)—a broad bean specialty of Quebec's Saguenay region and the principle ingredient of the iconic *soupe aux gourganes.*

GRANDFATHERS IN MAPLE SYRUP. See *grand-pères.*

GRAND-PÉRES (also called grandfathers in maple syrup)— a boiled doughnut popular in Quebec back when and now.

G

RECIPE

Grand-péres

Whisk together 1 cup flour, ½ cup milk, a pinch of salt and 2 eggs, and drop spoonfuls into a pot of maple syrup that has boiled and been turned down to a simmer. Cover the pot and simmer for 15 minutes, taking care not to lift the lid.

GRANELLO CHEESE—hard cow's milk cheese that is so reminiscent of Asiago and Parmesan it can almost transport you to Italy. It is crafted by the oldest family-operated cheese factory in Ontario, the Paron Cheese Company in Binbrook, a company that makes a wide range of single-herd cheeses.

GRAPE PIE—a crusted dessert pie popular among pioneers, made with wild fox grapes (*Vitis labrusca*). Nowadays it is mostly made from the grape's hybrid, the Concord grape, hybridized at Concord, Massachusetts, in 1849. To make, just pop pulp from grape skins and set the skins aside. Put pulp through a food mill or sieve to separate seeds, combine pulp and skins, pour into a baked piecrust, cover with top crust and bake. Do not ever refuse a piece of wild grape pie—it is heaven on a plate.

GRAYLING. *See* salmon.

GREAVES JAMS AND JELLIES—a brilliant selection of jams and jellies made the old-fashioned way at Ontario's picturesque Niagara-on-the-Lake since 1927 and available at specialty stores across Canada or online. Try their raspberry spread, 100 percent fruit and probably the best-tasting jam on the planet.

GREEN COD. *See* ling cod.

GREEN CORN—a once-common name for sweet corn and found as meaning that in many old cookbooks.

GREEN CORN PATTIES—fried sweet corn cakes made by pioneer settlers.

RECIPE

Green Corn Patties

Grate 1 pint of kernels from cobs of corn, mix with 1 teacup flour, 1 spoonful butter, 1 egg, and salt and pepper to taste. Form into cakes and fry in butter until golden brown.

GREEN CORN PUDDING—a harvest-time favourite with pioneer settlers.

RECIPE

Green Corn Pudding

Grate kernels from 12 cobs and set aside. In a saucepan, heat 1 quart milk with 1 lb butter and ¼ lb sugar. Beat 4 eggs fluffy and stir into milk a little at a time, alternating with corn. Bake for 4 hours, and when cooled, serve with a sauce made of butter, milk and nutmeg.

GREEN TOMATO CHOW CHOW—a Nova Scotia relish made by combining sliced onions with double the amount of sliced green tomatoes. Green tomato relishes, sauces and ketchups were popular all across Canada owing to the late ripening characteristics of older varieties of tomatoes. The relish is traditionally served with baked beans.

GREEN TOMATO SOUP—a Quebec original; green tomatoes boiled in water that contains onions, cinnamon, cloves, sugar and pepper, then combined with a roux of butter, flour and milk.

G

GROAT—cleaned, toasted and hulled grains crushed or steel cut into small pieces. Prior to 1877, when the American company Quaker Oats perfected a steam-rolling process, all oatmeal was groat that required soaking and long cooking times to soften kernels. Irish oatmeal is groat, while buckwheat groat is called kasha.

GROSSE SOUPE—a hardy Acadian soup resembling English hodge podge and made with beef shank, onions, beans, peas, green beans, potatoes, cabbage, turnips and corn, and flavoured with herbs.

GROUND CHERRY (*Physalius virginiana*; also called cape gooseberry)—a favourite with Canadian settlers, the ground cherry is a low-growing perennial commonly found at the edges of clearings and along roadways. It is a member of the Chinese Lantern family, with a cherry-sized fruit surrounded by a papery covering, and a taste reminiscent of plums and apples. Called *cerises de terre* in Quebec, these tasty, luscious berries were and still are prized for making pies, jams and jellies.

GROUND LEMON. *See* mayapple.

GROUNDNUT (*Apios americana*; also called potato bean)—not to be confused with its relative the peanut, the groundnut plant does yield similar-looking tubers that, when dried, have a taste reminiscent of peanuts. A climbing perennial native to

North American forests, the tubers were a major food source of native peoples and a lifesaver to many early Canadian settlers. Dried, the beans were ground into flour and used to thicken stews, extend wheat flour or make bread. Today, groundnuts are a popular forage food and high on the list of plants with a commercial future.

GUEDILLES—the base for lobster rolls, but any meat, fish, fowl or egg can replace the lobster. You mix chopped lettuce, tomatoes, green onions, salt and pepper with a good dollop of mayonnaise and your meat selection and serve it on a grilled hot dog bun.

GUMDROP CAKE—a favourite Maritime cake made by adding chopped gumdrops to a normal white cake recipe…sounds weird but tastes good, especially with chocolate ice cream.

GUNN'S RYE BREAD—a Winnipeg icon since 1937, Gunn's bakery somehow instills a sense of place into their glorious rye bread. One bite and you know you are in prairie country.

GUT PUDDING—a Prince Edward Island specialty sausage made by early settlers using a mix of cornmeal, leftover meat scraps and hard beef suet.

G

H

HABITANT PEA SOUP. *See* pea soup.

HABITANT BRAND SPLIT PEA SOUP—a national favourite since 1938, the year Montreal resident Phillip Morin moved to Manchester, New Hampshire, and canned up a batch of his daughter Marie-Blanche's pea soup and gave away free samples while warning people not to add water. Most Canadians are surprised to learn their favourite pea soup had its beginnings in the U.S., but in 1968, the brand came home when Canadian food giant Catelli bought the company, only to sell it two decades later to the Campbell Soup Company.

HADDOCK HASH—an iconic Nova Scotia mixture of haddock, cream, salt pork, potatoes and beets.

HALF-HOUR PUDDING—a simple pioneer dessert made as follows.

RECIPE

Half-hour Pudding

Cream 4 Tbsp butter and 1 pint sugar, then add 3 egg yolks and beat well. Add 1 cup cornmeal and fold in the whipped whites of the 3 eggs. Bake in a dish or ramekins and serve with molasses or maple sauce.

HALIBUT LOAF—a Maritime specialty that uses flaked, leftover halibut as a substitute for meat in a standard meatloaf recipe. In Canada's formative years, Maritimers thought cod as common-place a food as lobster and much preferred halibut.

TRIVIA

Halibut

Halibut (*Hippoglossus hippoglossus*) is the largest of the Atlantic flatfish. Sometimes weighing in at over 100 kilograms, it is normally fished in the 2–3 kilogram range and is called "chicken halibut."

H

HALL'S ORIGINAL SUCKER—a hugely popular lollipop of the late 19th and early 20th centuries. Uniquely Canadian and made at the Crystal Beach Amusement Park in Crystal Beach, Ontario, it has recently been reborn and is now made by the Crystal Beach Candy Company of Fort Erie, Ontario. It is available at the candy company, local retail outlets and online.

HAM IN MAPLE SAP. See *jambon de la cabane à sucre*.

HARD-TIMES PUDDING (also called *pouding de chomeur*, poor man's pudding)—a hasty, or cake and sauce, raisin pudding popular in Quebec, where the translation means "unemployed person's pudding."

HAWAIIAN PIZZA—said to have been invented in Canada in the mid-20th century, this pizza features back bacon (also called Canadian bacon in some parts of the world) and pineapple. Hawaii used to be the number one producer of pineapple in the world, hence the moniker—at the time, anything with pineapple in it was considered Hawaiian.

HAWKINS CHEEZIES—a popular, extruded fried cornmeal and Cheddar cheese snack food invented and manufactured by the W.T. Hawkins Company in Bellville, Ontario, since 1946.

HAZELNUTS (also called beaked hazelnuts, filberts)—the sweet nut or seed of the hazel tree (*Corylus cornuta*) and an important food source for First Nations and pioneer families.

HAZELNUTS

During pioneer days, beaked, or northern, hazelnuts were pressed for oil, roasted, boiled, candied, ground into flour to enhance Indian meal and snacked on while thinking of better days in the home country. Nowadays, hazelnuts are grown commercially in BC's Fraser River valley and are sometimes available in markets across the country.

HAZELNUT BREAD (also called hearth cake)—a fried mixture of hazelnut flour, cornmeal, water and maple syrup; an important food for First Nations and early settlers.

HEARTH CAKE. *See* hazelnut bread.

HEARTNUT—a seed sport (variation) of the Japanese walnut (*Juglans ailantifolia*), the heartnut is the variation *J. a.* var. *cordiformis*. The heart-shaped nuts are easily opened and better tasting than regular walnuts, and the tree takes to our southern areas like fish to water.

HEMP HEARTS—hulled seeds of the hemp plant (*Cannabis sativa*) that are a trademarked nutritional supplement of Rocky Mountain Grain Products in Lethbridge, Alberta.

HEMP OIL—exceptionally high in essential fatty acids, hemp oil is not only nutritional but also tastes good and makes a fine salad dressing. Produced near Winnipeg by Hemp Oil Canada, this product is available in some health food stores and online. The company also produces hulled seeds and hemp flour.

HERBES SALÉES—a mixture of salt-preserved herbs from the lower St. Lawrence region of Quebec and an important component of early Quebec and Acadian dishes. While there is no set recipe, *herbes salées* can include almost any herb—always fresh, never dried.

HERRING. *See* Atlantic herring. *See also* Pacific herring.

HERRING ROE—a long-time east coast delicacy, while on the west coast, First Nations harvested and cooked herring roe long before any Europeans arrived. Herring roe are historically a byproduct of the east coast fishery, while on the west coast, herring are caught explicitly for the roe, or the roe are harvested on kelp fronds in a sustainable type of aquaculture. *See also* ghow.

HICKORY NUT CAKE—a cake favoured by early settlers who gathered, dried and stored huge quantities of nuts during fall. Sweet and delicious, the nuts were toasted, salted and used for snacks, or chopped and baked into pies, cakes and cookies. They even saw use as chicken feed.

RECIPE

Hickory Nut Cake

Cream ½ cup butter with 1¾ cups sugar. Blend 3 cups flour, 3 tsp baking powder and a pinch of salt, and slowly add to butter-sugar mixture with 1 cup whole milk. Beat 6 egg whites stiff and fold into mixture along with 1 cup chopped hickory nuts and 2 tsp vanilla. Bake in 2 cake pans at 350° F for 30 minutes or until an inserted knife comes up clean.

HICKORY STICKS—a fried, hickory-flavoured potato stick manufactured by Hostess Foods, now a wholly owned subsidiary of Frito-Lay, and a favourite Canadian snack food.

H

Hickory

• Three species of hickory are native to southern areas of Ontario and Quebec, but only two—the shag and shellbark hickory—produce edible nuts. The latter (*Carya laciniosa*) is the most desirable owing to its larger, sweeter fruit.

• The hickory is a long-lived member of the Walnut family, has hard, durable wood and grows to considerable size; traits not missed by early lumbermen. During the first part of the 19th century, most of Canada's hickory trees were turned into tool handles and spokes for wagon wheels.

HIGHBUSH CRANBERRY JELLY—a tasty condiment made from highbush cranberries. While not particularly pleasing consumed fresh, the berries take to sweetening nicely and jell easily owing to high pectin content. A favourite of early settlers, the berries are prized by modern-day foragers who sell their jellies and jams at farmers' markets and through online specialty companies.

HIGHBUSH CRANBERRY WINE—a luscious, deeply flavoured libation made from the orangey-red fruit of the highbush cranberry shrub, common to most Canadian provinces.

HODGEPODGE (also called hotch potch)—a traditional Nova Scotia celebratory harvest stew with a name borrowed from the Scottish mutton stew. However, the Scottish stew pales in comparison, as the Nova Scotia version includes every ripe vegetable the family garden can offer up: onions, cauliflower, potatoes, squash, runner beans, peas, carrots, Brussels sprouts, broccoli, beets, turnips and parsnips. Stewed with a bit of salt pork, this mélange of plenty was and still is served aside beef or fish, or as a meat or fish stew.

HOMINY. *See* lyed corn.

HONEY—bee food, 38 percent fructose and 31 percent glucose, with about the same sweetness as granulated sugar. Honey is classified by source, and it can be monofloral, from one flower, or polyfloral, from many flowers. Canada has wildflowers in abundance: alfalfa, clover, buckwheat, loosestrife, canola, fireweed, blueberry, cranberry, blackberry, huckleberry, sunflower, basswood, vetch-flower from the foothills of BC's Monashee Mountains and the superlative borage from the Prairie Provinces. All flowers used by honeybees produce a variety of tastes that make Canadian honey the world's finest.

H

HONEY

Liquid, creamed or still in the comb, Canadian honey is a national treasure that should be guarded against depredation by foreign conglomerates. An Ontario company controlling a good percentage of the Canadian honey market and recently acquired by a U.S. firm has begun to cut their honey with a cheap import from Argentina. Read labels carefully and buy only 100 percent Canadian honey from co-op processors like the prairies' BeeMaid Company, or from farmers' markets.

HONEY BUTTER—a blend of honey and butter popular with early settlers and still available in specialty food stores. Orange, lemon or cinnamon is often added as additional flavouring.

RECIPE

Honey Butter

Combine ½ cup butter, ¾ cup honey, 1 Tbsp orange juice and 1 tsp orange rind. Lemon or cinnamon can be substituted for orange.

H

Honey

- With over a half million bee colonies, Canada is a major honey producer and ranks sixth in the world, with an annual harvest of around 30,000 tons. Roughly half comes from the Prairie Provinces.

- Honeybees were unknown in North America until their introduction by the French in the early 17th century. The bees soon escaped into the wild and established colonies across the continent. It was a good thing for settlers, as the wild colonies pollinated crops. Today, farmers cannot depend on hit or miss pollination and employ beekeepers that specialize in providing hives for servicing crops and orchards.

- Disease within honeybee colonies has always been a problem, but in recent years, Colony Collapse Disorder (CCD) has been decimating bee populations. One day the worker bees are busy pollinating and gathering honey, and the next they are gone. Some scientists blame a virus, others blame pesticides and herbicides, and still others say it is a combination. Whatever the reason, it has to be fixed soon or apiarists will begin switching over to unaffected Africanized bees, turning rural areas into dangerous no-go zones.

HOOP CHEESE (also called baker's cheese)—originally a soft cheese made by pioneers with skimmed milk and no added salt. It had a texture similar to baker's cheese. After being set with rennet, curd placed into a wooden hoop draped with cheesecloth was set aside until the whey had dripped out the bottom. When milk became plentiful, salt added to the curd for preservation and weights placed onto the hoops resulted in a denser, almost hard cheese with good keeping qualities. Hoops weighing about 20 pounds became so popular on general store counters that a cutter was invented to create wedges, a device you see sometimes at country auctions or antique shops.

HOPS (*Humulus lupulus* var. *neomexicanus*)—a native hop plant that produces cones or strobiles used by First Nations and early pioneers to flavour drinks, baked goods and meat dishes. Fresh, young leaves are a tasty addition to any green salad, and the plant made wonderful shading for front porches. Most important to early settlers was the hop cones' ability to host yeast and be a constantly available bread starter. The pioneers needed only boil a few handfuls in water, pour it still boiling into 1 L flour, strain, add a bit of old yeast starter when the mixture cooled and place it next to a fire until fermentation.

HORNE'S CUSTARD POWDER—Newfoundland's answer to Bird's Custard Powder and preferred by many bakers. It is now made by Select Food Products in Toronto and is distributed across the country.

HORSE BEAN (*Vicia faba*; also called Windsor bean, faba bean)—an ancient broad bean planted by pioneer settlers in maturing apple orchards to suck up excess ground moisture and prevent extraneous wood formation in the trees. Horse beans produce an upright plant with no tendrils. The large pods shell easily and yield five to seven quarter-sized beans. Used extensively by pioneer cooks, the beans lost popularity for a time but have been rediscovered by upscale chefs and heritage food gardeners.

HORSERADISH (*Amoracia rusticana*)—a perennial herb related to mustard and cabbage. The sauce is a tasty condiment deemed necessary by the very earliest English settlers, who planted horseradish immediately on arrival. Later settlers to Canada were delighted to find an even more potent horseradish growing in the forests, as the herb had escaped from gardens and spread into the wild. Young, tender horseradish leaves make a tasty addition to green salads or can be cooked like spinach. Grated and mixed with vinegar or lemon juice, horseradish was, and still is, a main condiment for oysters. With the addition of a little fresh mustard and sugar, it becomes an ideal condiment for roast beef, ham and seafood. Mix about a teaspoon of horseradish into a quarter cup of ketchup to make your own seafood sauce.

H

RECIPE

Horseradish Salad

Add 1 pack lemon jelly powder to 1½ cups boiling water. When the Jello begins to set, reserve ½ cup and set aside. Add ½ cup whipped cream, ½ cup mayonnaise and 4 Tbsp drained horseradish juice. Blend and chill. When set, cover with reserved lemon jelly and chill thoroughly.

HORSERADISH VINAIGRETTE—a lively salad dressing and a favourite of upscale Canadian restaurant chefs.

RECIPE

Horseradish Vinaigrette

Whisk 2 Tbsp each freshly grated horseradish and cider vinegar with ¼ tsp each salt and freshly ground pepper. Whisk continuously while slowly pouring in ½ cup canola or grape seed oil until dressing forms. Before serving, add finely chopped fresh parsley or chives.

TRIVIA

Horseradish

- Grated horseradish loses both colour and potency quickly. To counter this loss, manufacturers of bottled supermarket sauce will often formulate it with a bleaching agent, sodium bisulfate, along with a heat source, oil of mustard.

- Horseradish is grown commercially in both Ontario and Manitoba. Most of the crop is used to extract peroxidase, an enzyme used to detect HIV.

- Take care when grating your own horseradish; the fumes will make a grown man cry.

H

HOT ROCKS CHICKEN—a First Nations method of cooking wild fowl adopted by settlers and now used by campers to prepare a fall-off-the-bone chicken delight. First Nations used clay and hides, but modern campers have aluminum foil.

RECIPE

Hot Rocks Chicken

Wrap 4 or 5 rocks in aluminum foil and heat in a campfire for 1 hour. Place seasoned bird on a large sheet of foil with 1 rock in the cavity and the remainder around the bird. Wrap entire assembly in foil. Wrap again with 3 layers of newspaper, secure tightly in a black plastic bag and let sit for 5 hours. Scrumptious.

HOT SANDWICH—chicken, turkey or beef on a slice of white bread, topped with hot gravy and served with a side of peas. Americans will discount our claims to this ubiquitous diner dish, but my grandfather once told me a hot turkey sandwich was the last meal he ate before shipping off to World War I from Halifax in 1915—a long enough time ago to be part of our great food experience.

HOTCH POTCH. *See* hodgepodge.

HOUSE BUNKIN—a Lunenburg, Nova Scotia, specialty fish stew with salt cod, onions and cream sauce.

HUCKLEBERRY MUFFINS—huckleberries, both black and red varieties (*Vaccinium membranaceum, V. parvifolium*), grow profusely on the west coast. An important food source for coastal First Nations, the berries were quickly adopted by BC settlers and turned into luscious pies, jams, jellies and…muffins.

H

RECIPE

Huckleberry Muffins

Mix 1 cup each quick rolled oats and milk and set aside. In another bowl, mix 1 cup flour, 1 tsp baking powder, ½ tsp baking soda and ¾ cup brown sugar. In a small bowl, mix 1 beaten egg with ¼ cup melted butter and add to oatmeal along with dry ingredients. Stir only until moist. Fold in 1 cup huckleberries, pour into greased muffin tins and bake at 400° F for 15–20 minutes.

HUGGER-IN-BUFF. *See* Dutch mess.

HURT WINE—a Newfoundland alcoholic beverage made from fermented berries of any plant of the genus *Vaccinium*: blueberries, blackberries, bilberries and huckleberries. The 16th-century English called them hurtes (hurts) or hurtleberries; the word was changed by American settlers to huckle, as in huckleberry, while in Newfoundland they kept the word as a catchall for any dark-coloured berry. Newfoundland has a host of hurts: hurt pie, hurt pudding, hurt cake, hurt crisps and, of course, hurt wine.

HYDROMEL (also called *vin de miel*)—a fermented and filtered honey "mead" brewed by the Musée de Iabeille, a honey museum in Chateau Richer, Quebec. The museum brews around 20,000 bottles annually, and it always sells out.

H

I

ICE CIDER—the precursor of ice wine, ice cider is the fermented juice pressed from apples that have frozen, either intentionally or unintentionally, on the tree. A favourite of New France pioneers, ice cider has maintained a habitant presence through the centuries and nowadays is pressed commercially by a number of Quebec craft cider producers.

ICE WINE (also called eiswein)—an ultra-sweet dessert wine originally made in Germany and later produced in small amounts by wineries in other countries, including Canada.

ICE WINE

The production of ice wine is labour intensive and depends on freezing winter temperatures to concentrate sugars in the grapes. However, in most wine-producing countries, low temperatures over an extended period are rare, and winter labour is a problem. Canada has the freezing temperatures, but until the 1970s lacked the grape varieties necessary to produce ice wine. Canada is now the world's major producer of ice wines from many grape varieties.

ÎLE D'ORLEANS CHEESE—Canada's first cheese, first produced over 350 years ago on Île d'Orleans, an island in the St. Lawrence River near Quebec City.

ÎLE D'ORLEANS CHEESE

Popular in the 16th and 17th centuries as a dessert accompanied by sliced apples, Île d'Orleans cheese went out of production in the 1970s but has since been reintroduced by Les Fromages de Île d'Orleans and called Le Paillasson. Alas, the cheese is only available in limited quantities in a few Quebec cheese shops and on Île d'Orleans. If you happen to visit Île d'Orleans and the fromagerie, be sure to try their wonderful cheese in a galette, a buckwheat crepe prepared on the premises.

I

INCONNU (*Stenodus leucichthys*; also called coney, connie, shee fish)—a large, oily game fish found in rivers and streams of northwestern Canada. Touted as a firm-fleshed northern delicacy by outfitters, the meat is actually soft and oily and is best smoked.

INDIAN BREAD—an unleavened flat loaf, the dough being a mixture of Indian meal, dried berries, beans and various nutmeats.

INDIAN BREADROOT. See *pomme-de-prairie*.

INDIAN CANDY—salmon fillets hand rubbed with maple syrup and salt (kippered), then smoked over alder wood for an extended period.

INDIAN CELERY (*Ligusticum* spp.; also called lovage, wild celery, smallage)—looks, smells and tastes like cultivated celery, but it is not even a relation. It was a treat for the earliest east coast settlers who foraged Indian celery because it completed their mirepoix, the three ingredients intrinsic to French cooking. This carrot, onion and celery base was very important in French cuisine even in early times.

INDIAN CHOCOLATE (*Geum* spp.; also called chocolate root, water avens)—a perennial herb with a root tasting slightly of chocolate. Water avens were gathered and used by First Nations and settlers to make a hot cocoa–like drink.

INDIAN CORN. *See* lyed corn.

INDIAN CORNBREAD—an unleavened, boiled bread made from ground sweet corn and beans.

INDIAN CUCUMBER (*Medeola virginiania*)—a white, crisp, finger-sized root that tastes surprisingly like cucumber.

INDIAN GINGER. *See* wild ginger.

INDIAN ICE CREAM—soapberries are sweetened with sugar, blue camas or the juice of other berries and whipped like egg whites.

INDIAN MEAL (also called cornmeal)—baking flour made from rough ground corn and beans that sometimes contained crushed walnuts, hickory nuts or beechnuts. Created by First Nations and adopted by settlers, the name became synonymous with milled corn, or cornmeal. Indian meal was a pioneer staple for making bread, cake and pudding and for thickening stews. *See also* lyed corn.

INDIAN MEAL MUSH—cornmeal boiled until soft, around an hour. It may be eaten hot as a breakfast cereal, or cooled, sliced and served as a meat side.

INDIAN MEAL PANCAKES (also called Indian slapjacks)—pancakes made with cornmeal and fried on a griddle.

INDIAN MEAL PUDDING—a baked cornmeal dessert sweetened with molasses that originated on the east coast and moved west with early settlers.

RECIPE

Indian Meal Pudding

Boil 5 cups whole milk; mix 1 cup Indian meal with 1 cup cold milk, add 4 Tbsp butter and boil while stirring. Beat 4 eggs with 1 cup molasses or powdered sugar, add 1 tsp each ginger and nutmeg and stir the whole together until thick enough to pour into buttered ramekins. Bake at 350° F for 2 hours.

INDIAN RICE. *See* northern rice-root. *See also* wild rice.

INDIAN SLAPJACKS. *See* Indian meal pancakes.

INDIAN TEA. *See* Labrador tea.

INDIAN TURNIP. See *pomme-de-prairie*.

INSTANT MASHED POTATOES—created in 1962 by Canadian Department of Agriculture research scientist Edward Asselbergs as a convenience for campers and for military rations.

IRISH MOSS BLANC MANGE—a favourite Maritime delight.

RECIPE

Irish Moss Blanc Mange

Soak ¼ cup Irish moss in 1½ cups water until soft (15–20 minutes). Combine with 1¾ cup milk and a pinch of salt, and cook in double boiler until thick. Strain, add 1 tsp vanilla, pour into jelly moulds and chill. Great with sliced fruit.

ISINGLASS—gelatin made from the dried swim bladders of large fish such as sturgeon. A valuable trade product for First Nations, this gelatin was used by early settlers to make aspic and glaze meats for preservation.

I

TRIVIA

Isinglass

During the 18th and early 19th centuries, isinglass became a lucrative business for the Hudson's Bay Company, as the gelatin was much in demand by English breweries for fining (clarifying) beer. With the rise of the east coast cod fishery, isinglass became a valuable byproduct of that fishery and a much cheaper commodity. Around 1840, an American inventor, Peter Cooper, perfected a powdered gelatin from pigs' feet, but it proved too expensive. Then in 1890, a James-town, New York, resident, Charles Knox, perfected a cheaper, granulated gelatin and packaged it for retail sale. Not long after, May Wait, a housewife in Leroy, New York, mixed Knox's gelatin with sugar and powdered flavouring and called her new product Jell-O. May Wait sold her Jell-O brand to American marketing genius Frank Woodward, who in 1926 merged his multi-million–dollar Jell-O empire with Postum Foods, with that company later merging with J.L. Kraft to form the mega conglomerate General Foods.

J

JAM BUSTERS—yeast-raised sweet dough formed into balls, fried in lard, slit with a knife and filled with jam.

JAM-JAMS—iconic brown sugar and molasses, jam-dabbed cookies very popular with Maritimers.

JAMBON À L'ERABLE. See maple-glazed ham.

JAMBON DE LA CABANE À SUCRE (also called ham in maple sap)—a braised ham specialty of Quebec habitants since the early days.

TRIVIA

Cabane à Sucre

Starting in the 18th century, sugaring became a winter business for habitants all over Quebec. The habitant would stake out an area of forest rife with sugar maples, then he would build a cabin to protect himself and his sugaring pots, pans and pails from the elements. Occasionally, his family would journey into the forest to join him, and these visits were cause for great celebration. These joyful events continue to this day, having become something of a springtime tourist attraction in Quebec. People no longer have to make the arduous journey to the sugaring cabins on foot, as they can drive to the *cabane à sucre*, observe the sap gathering and the sugaring, and partake of a feast of pea soup, ham, tourtiere and maple taffy.

> **RECIPE**
>
> *Ham in Maple Sap*
>
> *Braise a whole ham for 3 hours in maple sap. Remove the rind and cover ham with a mixture of raisins, maple sugar, dry mustard, ground cloves and salt, and bake at 300° F for ½ hour.*

JEANNE'S CAKES—among the world's tastiest cakes and only available at Jeanne's bakery or supermarkets in Winnipeg...it's a crying shame.

JERKY—strips of beef or wild game that have been sun dried or salt cured.

JERSEY MILK BAR—the iconic Canadian candy bar creation of the William Neilson Company.

JERUSALEM ARTICHOKE (*Helainthus tuberosus*; also called topinambour, sunroot, sunchoke)—not from Jerusalem, nor an artichoke, but a North American plant tuber that resembles ginger root, with a taste similar to its namesake artichoke. First introduced to Samuel de Champlain by native peoples in 1605 and called Canadian potato by the French, the plant was so widely cultivated in France that it became almost an invasive weed. A relative of the sunflower and a staple food of early settlers, the crispy sunchoke makes a delicious addition to salads and stir-fries.

JERUSALEM ARTICHOKE FRITTERS (also called topinambour beignets)—sliced Jerusalem artichokes dipped in batter and fried golden brown.

Jersey Milk

The William Neilson Company was established 1893 as a back-of-the-house dairy and ice cream operation. As business improved, chocolate products were added as a way of providing winter employment to workers and disposing of unsold milk. Two decades later, the company was producing over 1 million gallons of ice cream and a half million pounds of chocolate products. In 1924, William's son Morden decided the time had arrived for a Canadian chocolate bar; insisting that only the finest ingredients obtainable be used in its production, he introduced the Jersey Milk chocolate bar to a grateful public.

Morden Neilson advertised his product as the best chocolate bar made. He was probably right; unlike the Hershey Company in the U.S., he used only high-quality cream from Jersey cows and refrained from adding soured milk to the formulation, which produces a product called "rotten milk chocolate"—and the not disagreeable, slightly off flavour associated with Hershey milk chocolate. Unfortunately, Jersey Milk bars are no longer made with the best Jersey milk, and one can only hope the present owners keep using the best chocolate in Canada's favourite chocolate bar.

J

Jerusalem Artichoke

Both the Jerusalem artichoke and the sunflower are members of the Daisy family, and mature plants bear similar-looking flowers. Introduced into English gardens by way of cultivators in Ter Nuesen, Holland, as girasole, or Italian  sunflower, the sunchoke from France, via Canada, was nicknamed Jerusalem to avoid confusion.

JERUSALEM ARTICHOKE SOUP—the iconic Canadian soup; made by the Mi'kmaq, adopted by the earliest French and still enjoyed across the nation.

RECIPE

Jerusalem Artichoke Soup

Cook thinly sliced leek, fennel and celery bulb in butter until soft. Add 1 lb peeled, thinly sliced Jerusalem artichokes, bouquet garni and 6 cups chicken stock; simmer until artichokes are tender. Cool soup, remove bouquet garni, add ¼ cup heavy cream and puree in small batches. Return to pot and reheat.

J

JEWEL JAM—a berry jam made from pitted cherries, gooseberries, raspberries and red currants. Popular with early settlers, the jam earned its name from the dab of ruby colour it provided to a bowl of mush.

JIGGS DINNER (also called *bouilli Canadien*, scoff)—a traditional Newfoundland dinner of salt beef, or salt pork, and vegetables.

JOHNNY CAKES. See *flan au blé d'Inde*.

JOS. LOUIS—a chocolate snack cake with a cream centre invented in Sainte-Marie-de-Beauce, Quebec, by bakery owner Rose Anna Vachon in 1932 and named after her two sons, Jos and Louis. Over the years, Vachon's little bakery grew into a successful family enterprise, making everything from jams and jellies to Granny's butter tarts, but in 2004, it was bought by the Canadian mega conglomerate Saputo.

JOSTABERRY—crossing black currant and gooseberry produces a thornless bush that likes our climate and has large clusters of black-blue berries that are excellent for making jams and jellies. Commercially grown in Alberta, cultivars are available from nursery supply companies for your garden.

K

KAMCHATKA LILY. *See* northern rice-root.

KENTUCKY FRIED CHICKEN—although the king of fried chicken, Col. Harland Sanders, did most certainly develop his secret blend of 11 herbs and spices in the U.S., both he and his secret recipe lived in Mississauga, Ontario, from 1964 until his death in 1980. The Colonel must have thought his "finger lickin'" chicken belonged here since his charitable fund, the Colonel Harland Sanders Charitable Organization, is still in operation and is based in British Columbia. It's a bit of a stretch to include the Colonel's chicken in the Canadian food experience, but since I once lived near the guy and knew him as a fine Southern gentleman who always had a big smile and a wave for neighbours, I thought I'd include him for old time's sake. Oh, and in one of the few conversations I had with the Colonel, while he was out watering his lawn and waiting for the cleaners to deliver his white suits, he told me the most secret ingredient in his mix was white pepper.

KERR'S BUTTERSCOTCH—a boiled, real butter and brown sugar candy made by Kerr's since 1895. Kerr's started out in St. Thomas, Ontario, moved to Brantford in 1898, and to Toronto in 1904. This all-Canadian family company produces a wide variety of quality candies for consumers, not the bottom line of financial statements.

KETCHUP (also called catsup, catchup)—in the very early days, ketchup was a fish sauce, then a mushroom sauce. It underwent another change around 1770, when American cook James Mease, who immigrated to Nova Scotia in 1782 during the American Revolution, concocted his popular tomato-based sauce. In 1876, an American from Pittsburgh, by the name of Henry John Heinz, called "Jack," began to bottle the ketchup that Canadians learned to love. When H.J. Heinz opened a plant in Leamington, Ontario, in 1909, his cooking vats could barely meet the demand. Today, the Heinz factory is streamlined and processes over 250,000 tons of fresh Ontario tomatoes into the ubiquitous red sauce. Heinz ketchup is available in plastic squeeze bottles, but their largest seller is still the skinny glass bottle that Jack made, the one that needs a pounding to get started.

K

KETCHUP AUX TOMATES ROUGES—a ripe tomato relish traditionally served in French Canada with *cipaille* and tourtieres, similar to chili sauce.

KIAK. *See* alewife.

L

LA TIRE. See maple taffy.

LABRADOR TEA (*Ledum groenlandicum*; also called wishakapuka, Weesukapuka, Indian tea)—a low-growing arctic shrub with leathery, furry leaves that, when infused in boiling water, produce a pleasant drink tasting of rhubarb. Popular with First Nations and English settlers, Labrador tea leaves are still being gathered from the wilds by people who relish the tea's pleasant taste.

> ### TRIVIA
>
> **Labrador Tea**
>
> Exported to England by the Hudson's Bay Company during the early part of the 19th century, Weesukapuka tea (the HBC trade name) became a taste-of-Canada sensation after young ladies discovered that an overindulgence of the herb would facilitate a cosmetic dilation of their pupils. However, it also made them sweat—an odious, sales-hampering side effect that soon put an end to exports.

LABRADOR TRAPPER BREAD—risen molasses bread packed with raisins, currants and butter and meant to last for weeks. Baked in quantity by Labrador trappers' wives, the loaves were the main ration of fur trappers making the rounds of their trap lines.

LAKE ERIE FRIED PERCH—a specialty item of restaurants from Quebec to Alberta, but mostly found on menus around Lake Erie, one of the best being the Erie Beach Motel in Port Dover, Ontario. Yellow perch (*Perca flavescens*) is one of our predominant freshwater fish species and can be found in lakes almost nationwide.

LAKE HERRING. *See* cisco.

LAKE TROUT (*Salvelinus namaycush*)—once the predominant species of the Great Lakes watershed, the lake trout has been decimated by lamprey infestation, habitat destruction and over-fishing. However, the fish maintains predominance in the North, where it is commercially fished and a star attraction for sport fishermen. Frozen lake trout from Saskatchewan, available in supermarkets across the nation, is both versatile and tasty fare.

LAMB'S QUARTERS (also called goosefoot, pigweed, fat hen, wild spinach)—brought along by some settlers as a garden plant, it promptly escaped into the wild to become a ubiquitous weed from coast to coast. That was bad for farmers but great for foragers, because leaves of the plant cook up to taste just like their relative, spinach. Lamb's quarters are delicious and, as the most foraged plant in Canada, are usually available at farmers' markets. The seeds, while tiny, are prolific and can be milled into flour. One day it may occur to people to stop battling this plant and start cooking with it. Try it fried with bacon and apples, and you will be out looking for more. Maritimers make a wonderful soup from lamb's quarters called weed soup, after one of the plant's common names: pigweed.

RECIPE

Weed Soup

Boil 2 quarts of only the tips of lamb's quarters in 4 quarts water for 3–4 minutes, then drain and coarsely chop. In a deep pan, fry 1 cup diced salt pork until crisp, then add 1 minced onion and cook until golden. Add 5 cups water, bring to a boil and add 2 diced potatoes and the chopped lamb's quarters. Return to a boil and stir in ½ cup oatmeal (not the rolled or quick variety). Simmer 30–40 minutes, stirring occasionally, and season to taste.

LARGE RAMPION. *See* evening primrose.

LASSY BREAD—Newfoundland yeast-raised sweet bread made with raisins, spices and molasses. Lassy is the Newfoundlander word for molasses, and it precedes many culinary creations.

LASSY MOGS. *See* mogs.

LAURA SECORD CHOCOLATES—in 1813, an American immigrant to our Niagara Peninsula named Laura Secord made a monumental 18-hour trek through the wilds to warn British troops of an impending attack by American soldiers. She was our very own heroine, but nobody had a clue she even existed until exactly one century later, when Toronto resident Frank O'Connor began making chocolates and putting her story on the back of every box. Laura Secord chocolates, along with the fame of our very own heroine, expanded across the country through outlets and drug store installations. In 1960, Ault Foods, owned by John Labatt Limited, bought not only the company but also the Secord homestead and turned the place into a tourist attraction. In 1983, Laura Secord was purchased by the English candy conglomerate Rowntree Macintosh, and in 1986, Rowntree was bought by the Swiss mega conglomerate Nestlé. Then in 1999,

L

Nestlé sold the brand to U.S. mega candy conglomerate Archibald Candy Corporation of Chicago, the makers of Fanny Farmer brand chocolates. In 2004, a consortium of financial giants, led by the U.S. investment group Gordon Brothers, bought and continues to run the company named for our heroine.

LAZY CAKE. *See* wacky cake.

LE CENDRILLON CHEESE—a chevre (goat cheese) made in St-Raymond de Portneuf, Quebec, by La Maison Alexis de Portneuf and judged world's best cheese at the 2009 World Cheese Awards.

LE CRU DU CLOCHER—award-winning, raw milk aged Cheddar cheese made at the Fromagerie au Village in Lorrainville, Quebec.

LE PIED-DE-VENT CHEESE—a well-ripened, semi-hard cheese made by the Fromagerie du Pied-de-Vent, on Quebec's Iles de Madeleine, an island in the middle of the Gulf of St. Lawrence. Le Pied-de-Vent is a raw milk cheese made from the milk of the original New France cow, the breed called Canadiennes.

LE RIOPELLE CHEESE—a rich, triple cream Camembert-style soft cheese made by a cooperative of five dairy farms on Quebec's Ile-aux-Grues and named for the famous painter and island resident Jean-Paul Riopelle.

LECHEVALIER MAILLOUX CHEESE—a soft, raw milk cheese crafted at La Ferme Piluma in St-Basile de Portneuf and judged the finest cheese in Canada by the Dairy Farmers of Canada in 1998.

LEMON CURD—an English delight made by settlers whenever the local general store received a barrel of lemons and the farm had an adequate supply of butter and eggs.

RECIPE

Lemon Curd

Juice 4 lemons into a double boiler along with 6 eggs, 2 cups sugar and ½ cup butter. Add the grated rind from 2 lemons, and whisk over boiling water for 20 minutes until thick. Pour into jars, cool and refrigerate. Lemon curd will keep for 3–4 weeks but is usually eaten after only a few days. Spoon it into pre-baked tart shells for a treat made in heaven.

LEMON HONEY—a faux honey made popular in the early days and made with easily acquired lemons.

RECIPE

Lemon Honey

Mix 4 oz butter with 1 lb sugar and 6 eggs, leaving out 2 whites. Grate in the zest and juice of 3 lemons and simmer until the consistency of honey.

TRIVIA

Honey

Contrary to popular belief, honey was not a foraged food item, as the honeybee is not native to North America. Beekeeping did become widespread, but since it required skill, it progressed across the country slowly.

LEMON PIE—iconic to the Canadian food experience since the early 18th century, when commercial cod shippers began voluntarily supplying their fishermen with citric rations from the Caribbean. Lemons and limes literally poured into our seaports,

L

including the ports of Quebec City and Montreal, and found their way into the interior by various routes. Scurvy was well known and dreaded, and to keep their men safe from the disease, pioneer women made sure to bake plenty of lemon pies.

LES BINNES. See *feves au lard.*

LICORICE ROOT (*Glycyrrhiza lepidota*; also called wild licorice)—grows from BC east to Ontario and was used by First Nations as medicine and sweetener. Pioneer settlers adopted the root to tame the piney flavour of spruce beer and as a flavouring ingredient for chewing tobacco. Wild licorice root is 50 times sweeter than sugar and has been considered by the province of Manitoba as a commercial crop to produce artificial sweeteners.

LINDEN TEA (also called basswood tea)—a therapeutic hot water infusion from the dried blossoms of the linden tree, also called the basswood or lime tree. French settlers were very familiar with the therapeutic qualities of linden tea and were delighted to find the tree growing everywhere.

LING COD (*Ophiodon elongus*; also called blue cod, green cod, buffalo cod)—a west coast ground fish found mainly off the coast of BC and the preferred quarry of scuba divers. Fished commercially but mostly caught accidentally, ling cod is a favourite of upscale chefs because the flesh is yummy, hangs together during cooking and plates pure white.

LINGONBERRY. *See* partridgeberry.

LIVER LOAF—a hard-times, Depression-era meal of chopped liver and mashed potatoes baked in a bread tin.

LOBCOUCE (also called flop)—a peppery Newfoundland soup made from salt meat, beef stock, shredded cabbage and onion.

Liver

Beef or calf liver dishes came into being during the Depression. Before the 1900s, the livers of slaughtered animals were considered toxic, and the organs were either discarded or fed to dogs. Hard times caused both homemakers and restaurant chefs to reconsider the lowly liver; dogs seemed to thrive on it, and the stuff sold for pennies a pound. Liver needed a placebo, a fantasy poison neutralizer, and when some bright chef hit onto soaking it in milk, the word spread through Canada and down into the U.S. like wildfire.

LOBSTER BENEDICT—substitute lobster for peameal bacon and you have a scrumptious favourite brunch dish of the Fairmont Algonquin Hotel in St. Andrews by the Sea, New Brunswick. Listed on the menu as Lord Selkirk's Lobster Benedict, the dish honours the memory of Thomas Douglas, 5th Earl of Selkirk, the Scotsman who brought 800 Scottish Highlanders to New Brunswick in 1803.

L

Fairmont Hotel

A rose is a rose is a rose even in the hotel business, as a name change from Canadian Pacific Hotels and Resorts to Fairmont Hotels and Resorts in 1999 changed nothing except the hotel conglomerate's international reach. The Canadian Pacific Railway built our grand hotels and now operates around the world in a manner that does us proud.

LOBSTER CHOWDER—a historic Maritime quick supper dish made by adding chopped lobster to a mixture of boiling milk, crushed crackers, butter and seasoning.

TRIVIA

Lobster

- Our Atlantic, or American, lobster (*Homarus americanus*) is a close relative to insects, in that they have exoskeletons and a jointed appendage. Lobsters are decapods, like crayfish, shrimp, crabs and prawns, which means they have 10 legs.

- Once considered a lowly food and a source of cheap fertilizer, the lobster has now risen to gastronomic stardom by way of good marketing, adventurous chefs and a government that understands resource management.

- Lobster trapped in warm, coastal waters moult their shells twice a year, while those hauled from deeper, colder waters moult only once and have denser, sweeter meat. The best-tasting lobsters in the entire world are hauled from the deep waters around Quebec's Magdalen Islands—it's worth going there for that reason alone.

- In 1885, Canadian lobster fishermen hauled in a record 100 million pounds of the delectable decapods; however, by 1918 the catch had dwindled to around 27 million pounds. Nowadays, through proper management, the annual catch has increased to around 35 million pounds.

- During both world wars, the government deemed components needed to manufacture fertilizer essential to the war effort; unable to acquire fertilizer, east coast farmers once again reverted to using wagonloads of lobster to fortify the land.

LOBSTER OIL—olive oil infused with fresh Atlantic lobster is a tasty drizzle for soups, salads and fish dishes. An inspiration of Vancouver chef Frederic of the Cannery Restaurant, the oil is sadly only available at the restaurant. You can try making it yourself with the shells gleaned during your next lobster boil.

> ## RECIPE
>
> ### Lobster Oil
>
> *Crush up shells, sans head, into 1 inch bits and dry in a 300° F oven for 10 minutes. Transfer dried shells to a saucepan, along with the coral if possible, cover with olive oil and heat gently for 3 hours. Strain and bottle the oil, and keep it refrigerated.*

LOBSTER PIE—a pastry-topped pie of lobster meat combined with diced potatoes, carrots, green peas and tiny white onions with a cream sauce base. Once an east coast favourite during penurious times, the pie has become the darling of upscale chefs.

LOBSTER ROLL—a long-time favourite fast food available almost anywhere on the east coast.

L

> ## RECIPE
>
> ### Lobster Roll
>
> *Mix 1 lb fresh or frozen lobster meat, chopped into bite-sized pieces, with ¾ cup mayonnaise, 3 Tbsp diced celery, 2 Tbsp minced onion and 2 tsp lemon juice, and serve on a hot dog bun.*

LOCHE ROE—eggs from the only species of freshwater cod. Loche are netted in the small feeder streams of the Mackenzie Delta solely for their delicious roe, while the remainder of the fish goes to the dogs.

LONG JOHNS—a long, fried doughnut specialty of Mennonite cooks and a much-appreciated snack at Mennonite-attended farmers' markets. *See also* fat Archies.

LOVAGE. *See* Indian celery.

LUNENBURG PUDDING—not a dessert, but a pork sausage with Germanic origins and iconic to Lunenburg, Nova Scotia.

LYED CORN (also called Indian meal, Indian corn, hominy)— a rough cornmeal prepared by First Nations, who boiled dried corn in an alkaline solution (water and ash) until the kernels expanded, thus freeing the hard skins. Thick, creamy and called Indian meal by Europeans, the product was dried and often mixed with nutmeats and berries.

TRIVIA

Lyed Corn

- Adopted by Europeans, lyed, or Indian, corn produced in small factories in Montreal was used by voyageurs, fur traders and settlers to prepare mush, a staple food of early Canadians. Fur traders headed west would take only three food items in their canoes: dried peas, salt pork and lyed corn. Settlers with wagons would take along barrels of Indian meal, along with corn seed and instructions on how to make more.

- When gristmills caught up with western expansion and ground cornmeal became available, settlers abandoned the making of lyed corn. However, old habits die hard and cornmeal kept the name Indian meal well into the 19th century.

L

M

MAC AND CHEESE WITH LOBSTER—ordinary American macaroni and cheese with an extraordinary Canadian twist: lobster.

MACKEREL (*Scomber scombrus*; also called Atlantic mackerel)— a small but prolific member of the Tuna family with oily flesh and a taste reminiscent of tuna. Mackerel are best when cooked fresh from the water, or brine cured and smoked like herring. During the early years of the 19th century, Nova Scotia fisheries shipped more than 50,000 barrels of cured mackerel per annum to all points of the globe, but nowadays, mackerel is mostly canned and available in all manner of sauces.

MACLAREN'S IMPERIAL CHEESE—a nippy cold pack cheese food invented in 1892 by Canadian cheese entrepreneur Alexander Ferguson MacLaren and his Imperial Cheese Company. Packed in porcelain containers, his product saw distribution around the world until J.L. Kraft acquired Imperial in 1920 as a vehicle to make and distribute his own patented processed cheese. The porcelain tub cheese went out of production until 1947, when Kraft Foods reintroduced the cheese in a red cardboard tub to test the effectiveness of television advertising. The test proved highly successful, and Kraft Foods was hard pressed to meet the sudden demand.

MANDRAKE. *See* mayapple.

MAPLE BUTTER—maple syrup cooked to softball stage, cooled and beaten until creamy; easily spread on bread or toast, it is long-time breakfast favourite.

MAPLE CREAM—a delicious maple spread for toast or sandwiches and a long-time favourite product of the maple sugar industry. Maple cream forms when the temperature of boiling maple syrup reaches 232° F, and you can make your own.

RECIPE

Maple Cream

Boil 2 cups fancy grade maple syrup to 232° F on a candy thermometer. Add ¼ tsp butter to keep the syrup from boiling over.

M

MAPLE DALE CHEESE—a century-old cheese maker with a brand new plant in Planefield, Ontario, Maple Dale produces many varieties of prize-winning cow's milk cheeses. The special emphasis is on aged Cheddar, with some six years old. Maple Dale's extra-mature Cheddar, a two-year-old variety, came away with the Grand Championship at the 2009 Royal Winter Fair in Toronto. The company will ship you cheese through online ordering, including curds made fresh daily.

MAPLE LEAF COOKIE—the all-Canadian sandwich cookie, shaped like a maple leaf, the filling flavoured with real maple syrup and baked by almost every commercial cookie company, the Dare brand being immensely popular.

MAPLE MOUSSE—a wonderfully light and fluffy maple dessert made even better with a dollop of whipped cream. It's like eating a sweet, maple-flavoured cloud.

RECIPE

Maple Mousse (*courtesy of Edna Staebler's* [Food That Really Scmecks] *mom*)

Soak 2 tsp plain gelatin in water. Beat 2 eggs, add 1 cup maple syrup and cook in double boiler for around 2 minutes while stirring. Cool mixture slightly, add gelatin and stir. When mixture cools and thickens, fold in 1 cup whipped cream, pour into serving dishes and chill. Serve with a dollop of whipped cream and dust with chopped nuts.

MAPLE PUFFS—maple syrup and sugar cooked to hardball stage, cooled slightly, mixed with beaten egg whites and nutmeats and spooned onto wax paper for cooling.

MAPLE SUGAR—maple sap cooked past the syrup stage to a thick molasses, whisked quickly until crystallization begins and poured into moulds. Another type of maple sugar and one preferred by First Nations and pioneer families was stirred sugar, wherein the syrup was continuously stirred until granulation. Stirred maple sugar more resembles regular sugar and will keep for longer periods.

M

MAPLE SUGAR CANDY—a common pioneer sweet made from maple sugar and dried nuts: walnuts, beechnuts, hazelnuts, chestnuts, etc.

RECIPE

Maple Sugar Candy

Place 1 cup maple sugar, ½ cup water, a pinch of salt and a dab of butter in a saucepan, and boil until brittle, about 300° F. Add 1 cup nuts, pour into a well-buttered tray and allow to set.

Maple Sugar

- Types of sugar: brown, burnt, caramelized, castor, coarse, confectioners, demerara, fondant, fruit, golden syrup, golden yellow, granulated, icing, liquid, liquid invert, molasses, muscovado, organic, pearl, plantation, powdered, raw, refined sugar syrup, refiner's syrup, sanding, soft, superfine, turbinado and...maple.

- Canada produces most of the world's maple syrup and sugar, with the province of Quebec supplying 80 percent of that amount. During the initial decades of the 20th century, Quebec's maple sugar production soared to meet the demands of the American tobacco industry, as it made an ideal flavour additive for cigarettes.

M

MAPLE SUGAR COOKIES—an iconic, easy to make pioneer cookie that is still in demand by hungry kids and dads across the nation.

RECIPE

Maple Sugar Cookies

Mix together 1 cup each flour, maple sugar and butter, 2 eggs, 2 Tbsp water, 2 tsp baking soda and, if needed, a little extra flour to make a soft dough. Drop onto cookie sheets and bake at 350° F for 15–20 minutes.

MAPLE SUGAR RUM—an alcoholic beverage made from fermented and distilled maple sap.

MAPLE SYRUP—from the boiled sap of silver, black and sugar maples, native peoples created an entire cuisine that became a huge benefit to early settlers. Wild game infused with maple syrup became a delectable treat, and corn mush sprinkled with maple sugar made that staple food bearable.

TRIVIA

Maple Syrup

- The Huron people used cold weather to make their maple syrup—they froze the maple sap, causing water to separate from the sugar solids.

- Maple sap is a misnomer, because what is tapped from trees is the sugary water that rises in the tree before the sap begins to run. When sap does rise, usually 18 to 20 days into the tapping process, harvesting ceases, because the sap smells and tastes like maple buds.

- In the old days, 90 percent of Quebec maple sap was boiled down into maple sugar and used as currency at local general stores. The stores would accumulate sugar and sell it to local dealers, who in turn sold it to Montreal wholesalers. In those formative years, maple syrup, called maple molasses, consisted of a thick liquid left over from the sugaring process.

- Today, syrup is king and Canada produces 85 percent of the world's supply from over 15 million trees—with each tree tapped by two spigots, that is almost one spigot for every Canadian. It's big business and good for rural economies, and consumers have a choice in what grade to buy. Canada #1 is graded as extra light, light or medium, referring to both colour and taste. The extra light has a light colour and delicate maple flavour, while the medium is a darker amber with a pronounced maple flavour, the supermarket maple syrup. Canada #2 is dark amber with a very pronounced maple flavour. It is usually only sold at the farm gate or at farmers' markets. Ontario also has a #2 grade for syrup sold at the farm gate. For culinary purposes, chefs want the #2 grades, but for your pancakes or ice cream, you'll want the #1.

M

MAPLE SYRUP PIE (also called *tarte au sucre*)—a centuries-old Quebec habitant and Acadian dessert pie made with ingredients common to those early days: maple sugar, syrup, butter, eggs, cider vinegar and flour.

MAPLE SYRUP SWEETIES—a once-popular children's candy made during the annual sugaring off. Mix the thickest syrup with fine flour, butter and a flavouring like lemon or peppermint and, when hardened, cut into small squares.

MAPLE TAFFY (also called *la tire*, snow taffy)—a taffy candy made by pouring boiling syrup onto snow and twirling the sweet onto a stick. In early Quebec, taffy pulls were attended by entire villages.

MAPLE VINEGAR—vinegar produced by boiling five pails of sap down to one, adding yeast, and fermenting the liquid in a cask. Several brands are available today, all from the province of Quebec and indispensable in the kitchens of upscale restaurant chefs.

MAPLE WALNUT ICE CREAM—one of our favourite flavours of ice cream enjoyed then and now and made with our most plentiful ingredients. Before the hand-cranked ice cream freezer came along, there was crème Anglais poured into metal trays and set on windowsills in winter, or onto a block of ice in ice-houses during summer. Canadian cooks still make this frozen delight, now called icebox ice cream.

MAPLE-GLAZED HAM (also called *jambon à l'erable*)—a Quebec habitant ham that once featured a glaze of only maple syrup and sugar, but is now made with maple syrup, mustard and brown sugar. It has become a nationwide favourite. See also *jambon de la cabane à sucre*.

MARITIME BROWN BREAD—iconic, down east leavened bread made with three flours (whole wheat, rye and corn) combined with buttermilk, molasses, salt and unsweetened applesauce. Traditionally served with baked beans, it is good anytime.

MATANE SHRIMP CHOWDER—a favourite of people from the Gaspe region of Quebec and made from the famous Matane shrimp harvested from the waters of the Gulf of St. Lawrence.

MATRIMONIAL CAKE (also called date squares)—a Mennonite butter and brown sugar cake with a date filling, customarily handed out at weddings and a favourite of all prairie residents.

MAYAPPLE (*Podophyllum peltatum*; also called mandrake, ground lemon, wild jalap, wild citron)—the fruit looks like a small lemon and tastes like a fig, but one bite of the root can kill you. This delicious fruit was cultivated by settlers but has been completely passed over by modern growers. Mayapples make an excellent jam and are much sought after by foragers.

MCINTOSH TOFFEE—a soft toffee bar invented in 1890 by Englishman John McIntosh. It became a favourite "in the trenches" candy of Canadian servicemen during World War I who, on their return home, set in motion a national love affair with the golden bar. In 1969, McIntosh merged with Rowntree, and the national love affair continued until 1988, when Rowntree-McIntosh was sold to mega food conglomerate Nestlé. In 2009, Nestlé stopped making the golden bar in hopes that the Canadian public will buy their poorer quality McIntosh one-bite wrapped toffees…an unlikely happening.

MEAT CAKES—a dinner mainly composed of meat chopped very fine, seasoned, mixed with egg and celery salt, pressed into cakes and fried in butter until crisp. They are an early version of Spam, but delicious and still popular in western provinces.

MEAT PIE (also called *pâté à la viande*)—an Acadian meat pie traditionally served at Christmas but now popular throughout the year. Originally a mixed game pie, *pâté à la viande* has evolved to include chicken, pork, domestic rabbit and some-times beef.

MEATBALL AND PIGS FEET STEW. See *ragout de pattes de cochon avec boulettes.*

MEATLOAF—an Acadian casserole dish evolved through wars and hard times to become a classic family favourite nationwide.

RECIPE

Meatloaf

Use your hands to mix 2 lbs ground beef with 2 minced onions, 2 eggs, 1 cup quick rolled oats or bread crumbs, 1 tsp grated fresh horseradish, 1½ tsp salt, ½ tsp pepper, ½ cup ketchup and 2 Tbsp Worcestershire sauce. Press into a loaf pan, cover with aluminum foil and bake at 350° F for 1½–2 hours or until the edges pull away from the pan. Remove foil for the last 30 minutes and brush with ketchup or barbecue sauce. Serve with mashed potatoes and green peas.

M

MICE COOKIES—a favourite Newfoundland snowball-type cookie made with butter, peanut butter, coconut, rice crispies, icing sugar and chocolate chips.

MIGNERON DE CHARLEVOIX CHEESE—almost as famous as Oka, this washed-rind, creamy, unpasteurized sensation is crafted by Laiterie Charlevoix of Baie-Saint-Paul, Quebec, from the milk of a single herd of Canadienne cows and aged to a finish by master cheese maker Maurice Dufor. Laiterie Charlevoix crafts a wide variety of single-herd cheeses available at specialty cheese shops; check online for sources.

MIKKU—caribou meat cut into thin strips and air dried; a historically important food for indigenous people in our Far North.

MILKWEED (*Asclepias syriaca*; also called wild cotton, wild asparagus, silky swallow wort)—cultivated by First Nations and gathered wild by legions of settlers, milkweed is a total utility plant, in that every part is used: flowers, leaves, pods and roots. If enough flowers are gathered, sugar syrup can be pressed out; the young leaves boil down like spinach and taste like okra; and young pods are excellent vegetable sides and make great pickles. In early spring, the roots are safe to eat and remind one of asparagus, but they are used mostly for their various medicinal qualities.

MILKWEED

Of the 20 or so species of milkweed, around half are native to Canada. Most are edible, but plants with white leaves are poisonous and should be avoided. Before consuming any parts of milkweed, be absolutely sure the species is safe.

M

TRIVIA

Milkweed

• Milkweed is the preferred plant of the Monarch butterfly.

• Silk from mature milkweed pods is too short for spinning into cloth, but mixed with wool or flax it produces a light, serviceable material. During the early 1800s, Canadian milkweed plantations provided material for lightweight hats. During World War II, milkweed silk, or floss, gathered by thousands of schoolchildren made a passable substitute for kapok in military clothing and floatation gear.

MILLHOUSE BARLEY—a new Canadian hybridized barley with grains that contain starch compatible with wheat in the flour milling process. Barley is more nutritious than wheat, and combination flours will increase the food value of commercial and home-baked goods. *See also* barley.

MILLION DOLLAR HAMBURGER—the burger specialty of Morton's Steakhouse created in the 1970s by Morton's partner, Klaus Fritsch, while a chef at the Montreal Playboy Club. One of the—if not *the*—world's best-tasting hamburgers, its secret lies in the quality of the ground sirloin and the hand mixing with raw egg, tomato juice, salt and pepper. Grilled to perfection, the burgers arrive with lettuce and sliced tomato on buttered, grilled buns—cheese or mushrooms are available on request.

MILSEAN CANDIES—superlative butter and demerara sugar toffees covered with Belgium chocolate and crafted by Sterling Rose Creations of Aldergrove, BC.

MINER'S LETTUCE (*Montia sibirica, M. perfoliata*)—two low-growing annuals or short-lived perennials native to British Columbia and much used by coastal First Nations, settlers and yes, miners, as salad greens. Still widely foraged, the greens are available at BC and Alberta farmers' markets.

MINT—First Nations across the country used the native variety, *Mentha arvensis*, both as medicine and for culinary purposes. However, pioneer settlers from Britain, fearful of being without adequate supplies of mint (including peppermint and spearmint) for sauce, tea and candy, brought along seeds to grow plants that promptly escaped into the wild, so nowadays most wilderness areas of southern Canada are awash in many varieties of mint. European mint varieties are grown commercially in almost every province for making jam, jelly and candy and for retailing in supermarkets. Wild mint is a treat, as the flavour is very pronounced; to find it, look for square stems.

M

MOCK CHERRY PIE—a prairie specialty, made before the railway enabled the purchase of fresh or canned cherries. Prairie cooks used cranberries and raisins to replace cherries and made respectable cherry pies.

MOCK OYSTER. *See* corn oyster.

MOGS—Newfoundland specialty cakes made with white flour, butter, sugar, baking powder and salt. If molasses is used instead of sugar, the cakes are called lassy mogs.

MOLASSES BREAD—a long-time east coast favourite. During the early 18th century, it used three readily available ingredients: cornmeal, butter and molasses.

TRIVIA

Triangular Trade

Until the middle of the 19th century, molasses, muscovado and maple sugars were the ubiquitous sweeteners in Canada, muscovado being an unrefined and sometimes half-fermented crystalline molasses used to distil rum. Canadian pioneer settlers enjoyed a plentiful supply of molasses and muscovado owing to the odious triangular trade in human beings. Molasses and muscovado from the Caribbean were sent to New England ports to be distilled into rum. A portion of the rum, along with molasses, muscovado and citrus, was sent on to Newfoundland to exchange for salt cod. Salt cod was then shipped Africa to exchange for slaves, who were then transported to the Caribbean to trade for sugars to make more rum.

M

MOLASSES CAKE—a molasses spice cake popular on the east coast.

MOLASSES COADY. *See* coady sauce.

> **RECIPE**
>
> *Molasses Cake*
>
> Combine 1 cup molasses, 1 cup sugar, 2 cups raisins, ⅔ cup shortening and 2 cups cold water and cook until thick, stirring constantly. Sift together 3 cups flour, ½ tsp salt, 1 tsp baking powder and 4 tsp cinnamon and combine with wet ingredients. Bake at 350° F for 45 minutes, or until a knife comes out clean.

MOLASSES COOKIES—an east coast favourite that spread across the continent in dozens of variations. They made 'em big, flat, small and fat, with some as big as your head with icing. Initially made only with molasses, this still-popular cookie now includes light brown sugar to temper the strong-tasting molasses.

M

> **RECIPE**
>
> *Molasses Cookies*
>
> Cream 1 cup shortening and ½ lb light brown sugar and mix with 1 pint each molasses and buttermilk. Stir in 6 cups flour and 1 Tbsp baking soda. Spoon onto baking sheets and pop into a 375° F preheated oven for 8–10 minutes.

MONT SAINT-BENOIT CHEESE—a mild, semi-soft Gruyère-type cheese produced at the Fromagerie de L'Abbaye Saint-Benoit, a dairy owned and operated by Benedictine monks in Saint-Benoit-du-Lac, Quebec. An aged, stronger-tasting version called Le Moine is also available.

MONTREAL MELON (also called Montreal market melon)—a cultivar of *Cucumis melo melo*, the muskmelon, which in the 19th century was a huge export crop for Quebec farmers. Montreal melons have a green flesh with a taste reminiscent of nutmeg, but it was their green flesh that almost caused their complete extinction when 20th-century demand for green-fleshed melons waned in favour of the pinks and reds of watermelon. Now a heritage crop, Montreal melons are grown by small farmers and are enjoying a comeback with upscale chefs.

MONTREAL SMOKED MEAT—the specialty of Swartz's, Dunn's and Lester's famous Montreal delicatessens. Melt in your mouth, chemical free, and every bite will make you wish you lived in Montreal.

MONTREAL STEAK SPICE—the flavour of old Montreal, blended and bottled by Club House Foods in London, Ontario, since 1990. For the answer to the question "why not London steak spice," you will have to ask the American owners, because the U.S. spice and flavour conglomerate McCormick & Company bought Club House in 1959. A popular spice mix, Montreal steak spice is shaken onto barbecuing steaks and roasts across the nation.

M

MONTREAL-STYLE BAGEL—Fairmount and St. Viateur are the Montreal bagel shops customers rave about, and for good reason. Both use wood-fired ovens to produce an extra crispy outside while maintaining a melt in your mouth centre.

TRIVIA

Montreal-style Bagels

American astronaut Greg Chamitoff took along Fairmount bagels for his six-month stay on the space station. He picked sesame seed bagels, and, although there is no report, a few seeds must have floated around and probably accounted for a few Marx Brothers antics.

MOOSE BURGER—an old-time favourite of pioneers and trappers, moose meat was chopped, fried and stuck into a sliced bannock roll. While the commercial sale of moose meat is prohibited, your chances of munching on a moose burger are excellent because over a million of the beasts wander around Canadian forests, and many thousands are harvested every year by hunters.

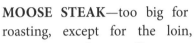

MOOSE STEAK—too big for roasting, except for the loin, moose meat is historically cut into steaks or cubed for stewing. Steaks should be dredged in flour, pan browned on both sides, topped with onion and garlic sauce and simmered for two hours, or until tender. In 17th-century New France, moose steaks were most often grilled and served with red wine sauce, the wine most probably Spanish, brought as ship ballast by Basque and Spanish fishing fleets.

MOOSEBERRY JAM—a specialty of northern Cree made from the bright red fruit of the low-bush cranberry (*Viburnum edule*). A sometimes ingredient in pemmican, the berries were an all-time favourite of early pioneers. Gathered and dried into loaves, the berries sweetened corn mush, glazed wild game and made wonderful pies, cakes and jam.

MOOSEHUNTERS DELIGHT—a favourite Newfoundland molasses cookie. *See also* molasses cookie.

MORDEN'S RUSSIAN MINT CHOCOLATES—a made-in-Winnipeg delight and the best chocolate mint in the world, a part of our Canadian food experience since 1959.

M

MOSSBERRY SAUCE (also called crowberry sauce)—a wild game condiment popular in Canada's Northwest. Big, blue-black and juicy, the berries are too bitter to be eaten fresh but are much used in sauces, jellies and pies.

MOUNTAIN SORREL (*Oxyria digyna*)—a wild, tender-leaved herb used extensively by western First Nations and early pioneers as a soup ingredient, flavouring agent and stew thickener. Young leaves have a pleasant citrus taste and have become a popular ingredient with upscale restaurant chefs.

MOZZARELLA DI BUFALA—authentic mozzarella cheese made from water buffalo milk by Natural Pastures Cheese Company in Courtenay, BC.

MUGWUMPS—mashed carrots and potatoes mixed with fried chopped onions and bacon.

MUKTUK—narwhal blubber; discerning gourmands may purchase a supply from Iqaluit Enterprises, Nunavut.

MULTI MILK—a concentrated milk for home consumption produced by Canada Dairies Corporation in Burgessville, Ontario, during the 1970s. It was a favourite of northern communities and Canada's military, but production ceased when Ontario fluid milk quotas pushed milk prices into the stratosphere.

MUSH—a thick, Indian or cornmeal porridge ubiquitous in the diet of early Canadian settlers. Settlers brought along barrels of lyed corn for making mush and seeds to grow more corn. For many Canadian pioneers, stewed rabbit and mush was an everyday meal for many years. Allowed to cool, mush can be sliced and fried—a welcome change to a gruelling diet.

M

MUSH PUDDING (also called Cream of Wheat pudding)—another "we have nothing else in the pantry" dessert common on the tables of early settlers. It's cornmeal, or Cream of Wheat, thickened in heated milk and beaten with eggs, sugar and spices.

MUSHROOMS—during spring and fall, our forests are a cornucopia of wild mushrooms: chanterelle, morel, king bolete, oyster and pine mushrooms abound. Pioneer settlers hunted wild mushrooms vigorously because they made wonderful soups and were a welcome addition to game meat stews. Nowadays, consumers are more likely to forage their mushrooms from supermarket shelves, and of those, the button mushroom is king. Canada produces around 110 million kilograms of these treats annually, with a quarter of that production shipped to U.S. markets. Never eat mushrooms harvested from the wild unless a mushroom expert attests to their safety.

MUSKOX—wild game meat from Canada's most northern communities of Nunavut and the Northwest Territories. The meat has a taste and texture similar to beef or bison and is prepared in a like manner.

MUSKOX MIPKUZOLA—air-dried muskox meat sliced thin like Italian prosciutto; a wild-game specialty product of Canada's most northern communities.

MUSSEL SOUP—steamed mussels in a broth made with butter, leek, celery, cider vinegar and seasoning.

MUSSELS—Canada's native east coast mussel is the blue mussel (*Mytilus edulis*), the bivalve found in net bags at local fishmongers and in supermarket display coolers and the species raised by our Maritime aquaculture industry by the millions. Blue mussels are native to both Atlantic and Pacific coasts, with the latter having only been recently recognized as a separate species. Mussels were once harvested from the wild but are now raised in long nylon mesh "socks" suspended from float lines; they receive all the benefits of a wild life without ever touching the sandy bottom. There is no grit in cultured mussels, the meat is plumper and the shell thinner, and they come clean and ready for the pot. Good eats, these delectable farm-raised bivalves.

TRIVIA

Blue Mussels

Blue mussels are a long-time favourite of seafood lovers around the world. Around 37 million pounds are harvested annually, with PEI accounting for 80 percent of Canada's total production.

MUSTARD—Canada is the world's largest exporter of mustard seed, supplying 90 percent of world demand. The Prairie Provinces grow three types of mustard seed: white, for making yellow ballpark mustard; brown, an extra-strong variety for making Dijon mustard; and yellow for making Oriental-style mustards. In Europe, farmers grow a variety of brown seed called black mustard that is used for making strong-tasting European-style sauce. *See also* charlock.

M

TRIVIA

Mustard

- Mustard was originally the name of the condiment, not the plant.
- Mustard oils are extracted from ground brown seeds.

MUSTARD PICKLES—a national favourite since pioneer days.

RECIPE

Mustard Pickles

Sprinkle 2 Tbsp pickling salt over 8 or 9 thinly sliced, large cucumbers and 4 cups thinly sliced onions, and allow to stand overnight. In the morning, drain the mixture and pop it into a large pot, cover with water and boil for 3 minutes; drain. Mix together 2 cups each vinegar and sugar (reserve a bit of vinegar to make a flour paste), and add 1 Tbsp turmeric, 1 Tbsp dry mustard and ½ tsp celery seeds. Mix reserved vinegar with 2 Tbsp flour and make a paste. Add the paste to the liquid mixture along with cucumbers and onions, bring to a boil and pour into sterilized Mason jars.

M

N

NANAIMO BAR—an iconic, three-layer, diet-busting confection consisting of a bottom layer of butter-soaked graham crackers, a creamed pudding centre and topped by a thick layer of chocolate. Invention claims abound; most credit the British Columbia city of Nanaimo, with only a few alluding to a New York café called the Nanaimo.

NANNYBERRIES (*Viburnum lentago*; also called sheepberries, sweet viburnum, wild raisins)—edible drupes of the shrubby nannyberry tree used extensively by First Nations to flavour pemmican and for a snack food. Dried berries make a passable substitute for raisins and were often used by pioneer settlers for baking, jelly making and snacking.

NATURAL PASTURES SOFT CHEESES—brie, camembert and triple cream camembert to die for, made from only the finest cow's milk in Courtenay, BC. Natural Pastures also makes farmer, water buffalo mozzarella and specialty cheeses. Look online for sources.

NETTLE SOUP—a surprisingly tasty and richly flavoured soup made from the tender tips and first two leaves of the stinging nettle plant (*Urtica dioica*). It is simple to make, unless you forget to wear gloves while picking the tips.

RECIPE

Nettle Soup

Heat 2 quarts of nettle tips picked in early spring, 1 pint beef stock, 2 handfuls oatmeal, a dollop of milk and a bay leaf, and season to taste with salt and pepper.

NEWFOUNDLAND BLOOD PUDDING—a favourite any-time sausage made to a European recipe, but with added oatmeal, onions and spices.

NEWMAN'S PORT WINE—Newman's, an early English trading company engaged in the lucrative codfish trade, discovered quite by accident in 1679 that port wine matured faster and better when left in St. John's, Newfoundland. They built extensive aging vaults under the city, and until 1914, St. John's was a major hub in Newman's port wine business. Newfoundlanders came to love Newman's port and not only drank it but also used it for culinary purposes. Today, Newman's port wine still portrays a picture of Newfoundland on labels, but as of 1996, EU regulations caused them to remove the words, "matured in Newfoundland." However, the vaults still remain and have become a tourist attraction.

NORTH GOWER CHEESE—produced by a marvellous little dairy farm in North Gower, Ontario. Cheeses are made from milk produced by their own Swiss Brown cows, which produce better milk than the common Holstein. Alas, the cheesy wonders from the Swiss cows are only available at the farm's store.

NORTHERN RED PRAWNS. *See* prawns.

NORTHERN RICE-ROOT (*Fritillaria camschatcensi*; also called Eskimo potato, Indian rice, Kamchatka lily)—a wet meadow plant once extensively cultivated by BC First Nations for its tuber. Eaten raw, the tubers taste like hazelnuts.

NOUGABRICOT—a preserve of apricots, almonds and pistachios that is popular in Quebec.

NOVA LOX. *See* Nova Scotia lox.

NOVA SALMON. *See* Nova Scotia smoked salmon.

NOVA SCOTIA LOX (also called nova lox)—a filleted salmon lightly cured in a mixture of salt, sugar and spices and not smoked.

NOVA SCOTIA SEA PARSLEY. *See* sea parsley.

NOVA SCOTIA SMOKED SALMON (also called nova salmon)—a filleted salmon cured in a mixture of salt, sugar and spices and either hot or cold smoked. Cold smoking does not cook the fish; it only adds flavour, and it is the usual preparation method.

N

NUNS' FARTS. See *pets de soeur*.

NUT BREAD—a "chock full of nuts" delicious wheat or Indian meal bread that uses molasses for a sweetener. Popular with early settlers, nut bread was baked during the autumn months when the forests became a cornucopia of sweet nutmeats. It is made with a normal bread recipe, but with a tad less flour replaced with crushed and floured nutmeats. Today, nut bread is still a delicious treat, especially if honey is used in place of molasses.

CANADIAN NUTS

Nut trees were plentiful in Canadian forests: walnut (black and white), beech, hazel, hickory and chestnut.

NUT BUTTER—dried nutmeats ground to a fine paste using a mortar and pestle, blender or food processor. Sweeten with honey or maple syrup, season and store in the refrigerator or a cool place.

NUT CANDY—a sinfully delicious brittle, or brickle, popular then and now. It is one of our most historical sweets.

RECIPE

Nut Candy

Combine 1½ lbs brown or muscovado sugar, 1 pint molasses, ¼ lb butter and 1 Tbsp vinegar and boil to the brittle stage. Pour mixture over toasted nutmeats spread over the bottom of a well-buttered pan. Once it cools, break it into bite-size pieces.

N

NUT OIL—an important source of cooking oil for settlers. Walnuts, acorns, beechnuts and hazelnuts were gathered, dried, cracked and pressed in such quantity that they provided settlers with much-needed income because the oils could be traded for goods at general stores.

O

OATCAKES—classic Scottish pancakes made with steel-cut Scottish oatmeal, flour, water, salt and yeast. They became a Canadian classic by the substitution of rolled oats and the addition of baking powder and sugar.

OATMEAL BOUCHIES—leftover porridge pressed into ramekins and turned out when cooled. Scoop out the centres, fill with berries or fruit and serve with cream.

OATMEAL BREAD. *See* porridge bread.

OILNUT SOUP. *See* butternut soup.

OKA CHEESE—a semi-soft, cow's milk cheese manufactured at the Fromagerie de L'Abbaye Saint-Benoit, a dairy owned and operated by Trappist monks in Saint-Benoit-du-Lac, Quebec. The flavour and texture of Oka is reminiscent of Port du Salut, an equally famous cheese made in France by monks of the same religious order. Oka-style cheese is also a product of the Trappist monastery in Holland, Manitoba.

ONION SHORTCAKE—an Acadian onion and cheese dinner cake popular in the Maritimes and the U.S. state of Louisiana.

ONION SOUP—a simple onion and meat stock soup of French origin, but made Canadian by the addition of croutons and cheese.

OOLICHAN. *See* eulachon.

OREILLES DE CRISSE (also called fried pig ears, smoked pork jowls)—deep-fried pork jowls with maple syrup; a common menu item of Quebec maple sugar shack tours, but tourists usually receive pork cracklings.

OVEN HEAD SMOKED SALMON—Bay of Fundy salmon cold smoked 40 hours using maple chips brought in from Quebec. Owners Joe and Debbie Thorne have followed this recipe for success religiously—you will have a divine experience when you taste their scrumptious products. Order online or, better still, take a trip to Bethel, New Brunswick, and buy right from their shop. That way, you can then drive around the corner to Ozzie's Lunch and partake of Rose Anne Waite's to-die-for fried clams and lobster rolls.

OVERSEAS FUDGE—a 1940s-era trick dessert made by boiling unopened cans of sweetened condensed milk until the contents turned brown and fudge-like.

O

OVERSEAS FUDGE CAUTION

Do not attempt to duplicate this treat—modern cans with quick-open tops are unable to withstand the internal pressure created during extended boiling.

OXEYE CAPERS—pickled unopened flower buds of the oxeye daisy (*Leucanthemum vulgare*), which resemble true capers but have a milder flavour. Introduced from Europe in the 18th century, the oxeye daisy has spread across Canada and is now considered an invasive weed.

OYSTER PLANT. *See* salsify.

OYSTER SOUP—a special-occasion dish for pioneer families, usually reserved for New Year's or Christmas suppers. In recent times this tasty dish has seen revival by upscale chefs.

OYSTERS ON THE HALF SHELL—fresh, plump oysters served on their shells with perhaps a squirt of lemon or a dab of grated horseradish are a gourmet delight more Canadian than butter tarts. John Cabot's triumphant 1497 roundtrip to the New World and his report of fish so plentiful you could haul them out with baskets caused French, Basque and Portuguese fishing fleets to beeline across the pond and cast their nets. Almost 100 years later, Champlain made a note in his log on the number of fishing boats he encountered at the mouth of the St. Lawrence River—a thousand, he wrote, but he was prone to exaggeration. Many fishermen dried fish on the shore and had friendly relations with the Mi'kmaq, the indigenous people of the area who loved to trade for European beads, mirrors and iron pots. Fascinating people, the Mi'kmaq: accomplished fishermen and good at getting the best deal, they would host banquets for their European friends and stuff them full of baked fish, tender moose fillet, seafood chowders and fresh oysters on the half shell while dickering for trade goods.

O

OYSTER IDENTIFICATION

• **Malpeque oysters** derive their name from Malpeque Bay on the north shore of Prince Edward Island. After being judged the world's best oyster at the 1898 Royal Exposition in Paris, all PEI oysters, farmed or wild, are called Malpeques. Around 10 million of the tasty bivalves are harvested annually. Malpeques are round shelled and juicy, and have a delicate texture.

• Another famous PEI oyster is the **Raspberry Point**, a smallish oyster with a salty flavour and sweet aftertaste.

• **Belon oysters**, imported from France and raised by aquaculture in Nova Scotia waters, are flat shelled with a nutty taste.

• **Beausoleil oysters** hail from New Brunswick, have a small shell and taste very delicately of the sea.

• **Caraquet oysters**, also from New Brunswick waters, are small and round and taste similar to Malpeques, but they are slightly less salty.

• **Village Bay oysters**, farmed in Bedec Bay, New Brunswick, are an easy-open bivalve with a well-balanced, salty taste.

• **Bras D'Or oysters**, farmed in the salty water of Bras d'Or Lake in Nova Scotia, are plump, slightly salty and sometimes a rarity in oyster bars owing to their susceptibility to diseases.

• **Shediac oysters**, harvested from Shediac Bay in Northumberland Strait and all but wiped out by disease, are making a slow comeback.

Our east coast oysters (*Crassostrea virginici*) not only carry famous names of origin, but also are subdivided into boutique names; e.g., a Malpeque oyster farmed in Colville Bay, PEI, will be called a Colville Bay at oyster bars.

British Columbia accounts for 60 percent of Canadian oyster production. All, except the tiny Olympia, are species imported specifically for aquaculture: Japanese, Yesso or Cupped varieties, the most favoured being the succulent, briny Kusshi, a Japanese oyster.

TRIVIA

Oysters

During the early days of the 19th century, PEI and Nova Scotia farmers began using oysters as free fertilizer to lime their fields, and the bivalve population suffered. By mid-century, packing companies had sprung up in those provinces. Properly packed oysters travel well, and with the opening of the Rideau Canal in 1832, oysters made the trip all the way from the east coast to Toronto on a regular basis. With the advance of railways, inexpensive oysters became a regular item with fishmongers nationwide. By 1870, the best Maritime oyster beds had been worked to exhaustion, prices for the tasty bivalve skyrocketed and restaurants stopped offering diners oysters by the quarter- or half-barrel (200 in a barrel). But the demand remained high, and by 1890, the packing companies were shipping out 35,000 barrels of the soon-to-be famous Malpeque oysters. In 1898, seafood judges at the Paris Exposition declared Canada's Malpeque oyster the finest in the world, and demand soared. Then in 1913, disaster struck; remaining Malpeque populations were decimated by a virus called Malpeque oyster disease, and our oystermen were out of business. But in the 1930s, the federal Fisheries Department hired Dr. A.W.H. Needler, a zoologist, to study the problem and find a fix. Although he never found a cure for the disease, he did save the tasty bivalve for future aficionados by searching out resistant oysters, reestablishing beds and plotting a course for aquaculture, a process that today yields almost 10 million kilograms of oysters annually from both east and west coast fisheries.

O

P

PABLUM—a popular baby cereal invented in 1930 at Toronto's Hospital for Sick Children by doctors Alan Brown, Teddy Drake and Fredrick Tisdall as a preventive for rickets. Good for kids, but moms soon found Pablum a useful ingredient for breads and muffins.

RECIPE

Pablum Muffins

Sift together ¾ cup flour, 2 tsp baking powder, ¼ tsp baking soda and ½ tsp salt, and mix with 1½ cups Pablum. Cream 1 Tbsp each sugar and corn syrup with 2 Tbsp butter. In a medium bowl, beat 1 egg into 1 cup milk and add creamed mixture; then stir into Pablum mix. Pour into muffin tins and bake at 375° F for 25–30 minutes.

PACIFIC HERRING (*Clupea pallasii*; also called sardine)— once the cornerstone species of the west coast fisheries, this species has suffered massive decline from overfishing and roe harvest.

PACIFIC HERRING

Until 1967, Pacific herring were the main component in the odious reduction fishery, where most of the harvest saw processing, or reduction, into fishmeal, oil and fertilizer. In the 1960s, the herring fishery turned to using purse seine nets that enabled quarter million–ton catches and led to inevitable consequences. In 1967, the Pacific herring fishery collapsed, and our government declared a four-year moratorium on commercial herring fishing. While the moratorium ran its course, herring fishermen turned to catching other species, and after four years, only the big-money fishing conglomerates, eager to capitalize on our Atlantic fisheries' successes with herring roe, were able to reestablish the reduction fishery. Nowadays, Pacific herring are caught for their eggs (the roe), while the fish sees reduction into meal to feed farmed salmon. BC Packers, owned by George Weston, and the Canadian Fishing Company (Canfisco), owned by advertising mogul Jim Pattison, are the major players in the west coast roe fishery, with each company raking in huge profits from the sale of salted roe to Japanese distributors.

P

TRIVIA

Pacific Herring

Of interest is the average size of today's Pacific herring compared to measurements recorded during the mid-20th century: today's fish are half the size, a phenomenon attributed to the removal of large fish from herring populations.

PACIFIC SALMON. *See* salmon.

PACIFIC SARDINE. *See* pilchard.

PAIN D'HABITANT—iconic Quebecois white bread baked in brick or stone ovens well into the 19th century. During the 18th and 19th centuries, bread made from white flour instead of Indian meal became a coveted status symbol.

TRIVIA

Pain d'Habitant

In 17th-century Quebec, home bake ovens were a symbol of freedom, since back in France, pay for play communal ovens were the law of the land.

PAIN PERDU (also called French toast)—thick slices of bread soaked in milk and egg by French cooks as a way to use up stale bread. This rather blasé breakfast dish underwent a culinary transformation in the New World when it met up with maple syrup for a match made in heaven.

PAL O' MINE BAR—a fudge and coconut chocolate bar made by Ganong Bros. of New Brunswick and a Canadian favourite since 1920.

PAN DADDLINGS—fried cakes similar to Newfoundland damper cakes, but deep-fried.

RECIPE

Pan Daddlings

Mix 2 parts rough milled rye flour, 1 part Indian meal, suet and a touch of allspice. Add milk to thin, and sweeten with 1 cup molasses. Deep-fry in hot oil.

PANCAKE BALLS—an east coast favourite and easy to make.

> **RECIPE**
>
> ***Pancake Balls***
>
> *Mix 2 cups each flour and milk with 3 egg yolks, 3 tsp sugar and ½ tsp salt. Beat the egg whites and fold into the flour mixture. Place a bit of fat in each depression of a muffin tin and fill to ¾ full with batter. Top each with cranberry sauce or jam, bake at 350° F until bubbles form, then turn and cook on the other side.*

PAPER BREAD—a thin cornbread made by rubbing a handful of cooked cornmeal gruel across a hot rock or fry pan.

PARKIN—an English molasses and ginger cake, but naturalized into our east coast cuisine by the substitution of rolled oats for cut oats, no ginger and more egg and butter...an oatmeal cake, sometimes sweetened with maple sugar.

PARSNIP FRITTERS—boiled and mashed parsnips mixed with flour, butter and seasonings and drop fried. While not a native plant, the parsnip was a recommended "bring with you" crop for early settlers and was used in dozens of recipes.

P

PARTRIDGE AND CABBAGE PIE—a game bird casserole or crusted pie with the main ingredient being spruce partridge, ruffed grouse or ptarmigan, all game birds common along the entire length of the St. Lawrence River. French explorer Jacques Cartier brought the minor ingredient, cabbage, to the New World in 1540, where it soon became as ubiquitous as the game birds.

PARTRIDGE IN GRAPE SAUCE—sautéed pieces of small game birds simmered in a white sauce with the wild grapes that grew on the east coast and along the St. Lawrence River.

PARTRIDGEBERRY (*Vaccinium vitis-idaea*; also called lingonberry, squashberry, fox-berry)—a close relative of the cranberry, but found on bushes up to 4 metres high. The brilliant red berries are widely foraged on the east coast to make jams, jellies and wines that are often mixed with bakeapples. *See also* wintergreen.

PARTRIDGEBERRY PUDDING (also called squashberry pudding)—a Newfoundland cake dessert usually topped with a rum and butter sauce. The cake recipe travelled west with early settlers and was adapted to include whatever fresh berries were handy: saskatoons, blueberries, raspberries, etc.

PARTRIDGEBERRY WINE. *See* squashberry wine.

PASTA—of Chinese origin, improved by Italians and made perfect by the inclusion of semolina flour made from Canadian durum wheat in the recipe. The finest pasta wheat in the world grows on our prairies, and we plant over 5 million acres to satisfy world demand. Even the Italians buy our durum wheat; in fact, they are our best customers.

P

RECIPE

Pasta

Break 7 eggs into a large bowl and whisk. Continue whisking while adding 4½ cups durum semolina flour and 2 tsp salt. When too stiff to whisk, turn out onto a floured surface and knead dough for 4–5 minutes. Cover dough with a damp towel, and let it rest for 1–2 hours. Cut into four parcels and run through pasta machine.

PÂTÉ À LA RAPURE. See rappie pie.

PÂTÉ À LA VIANDE. See meat pie.

PÂTÉ AUX BUCARDES. See clam pie.

PÂTÉ AUX MOUQUES—an Acadian mussel and potato pie still popular in parts of the Maritimes and Quebec.

PÂTÉ CHINOIS (also called Chinese pie, shepherd's pie)— ground beef, corn and whatever vegetables seem apropos, topped with mashed potatoes and baked. It's called Chinese pie because during the late 19th century, many Quebecois men travelled to the U.S. state of Maine to work in the mills, and at one mill town called China, they discovered shepherd's pie and returned home with the recipe. While not an original part of the Canadian food experience, *pâté chinois* has existed in Quebec so long and in so many variations that it must be included.

PÂTÉ CROCHES—a pork turnover or pasty specialty of Ile aux Coudres, an island off Baie-St-Paul in the Charlevoix area of Quebec.

PAWPAW (*Asimina triloba*)—a tree native to North America and once common to the north shores of Lake Ontario and Lake Erie. It produces the largest fruit on the continent, and the fruit was commercially harvested during the early 18th century. A relative of the more southern custard apple and tropical cherimoya, the fruit has a creamy texture with a taste reminiscent of banana, pineapple and mango.

PEA SOUP (also called French Canadian pea soup, habitant pea soup)—a historic Quebecois soup made from dried green or yellow split peas and a ham bone. Originally an Acadian soup with salt pork, it now has many recipe variations, but most include a ham bone.

P

RECIPE

Pea Soup

Start with a meaty ham bone and cover with water in a stockpot, throw in a chopped onion, some dill, chives and parsley, and boil. Place 1½ cups dried split peas in  *a bowl, add boiling water to cover the peas, then cover the bowl with a lid and allow to stand for softening. When the water in the stockpot is down by one-third, remove bones and fat. Cube 3 potatoes and add to soup along with extra ham, salt and pepper, and simmer until potatoes are soft. Enjoy.*

TRIVIA

Pea Soup

- During Champlain's fourth voyage up the Ottawa River, he was much surprised to find the local Iroquois growing French peas. He was even more surprised to find that the peas grew larger and had superior taste. French garden peas had found a paradise in Canada.

- Contrary to popular belief, pea soup did not originate in Quebec; it immigrated to that province from Europe through foggy ("a pea souper day") Newfoundland. "It's the devil's birthday again," was a Newfoundlander's greeting to another day of pea soup. The French fishing fleet plied the Newfoundland coast years before Champlain made his historical visits, and they consumed large quantities of soup made from easily transported dried peas and salt pork.

PEACH CHUTNEY—a condiment originating in British-ruled India but nationalized by substituting fresh peaches for mangos.

P

TRIVIA

Peaches

In 1870, farmers around the western shore of Lake Ontario were harvesting and shipping over 70,000 bushel baskets of peaches from 6 million trees. Around 1880, the peach trees were struck by a virus that wiped out half their number, and an unusually hard winter of 1898–99 wiped out almost all that remained, so farmers turned to growing other fruits and grapes. Today's peach tree,  a hybrid, is better able to withstand disease and weather and is once again a main crop of Ontario fruit growers and also growers in BC's Okanagan Valley.

PEAMEAL BACON (also called Canadian bacon)—an iconic slab of lean, cut-from-the-loin and cooked bacon coated with yellow corn meal. The baked or boiled peameal bacon supper was a settler's dish during early fall when hogs were butchered and the bacon plentiful. Often confused with cured and smoked back bacon, peameal is brine cured and more resembles ham.

P

RECIPE

Canadian Baked Eggs

Lay slices of peameal bacon in buttered ramekins. Break 2 eggs side by side in each ramekin. Sprinkle with Cheddar cheese, bake at 325° F until the whites are set, then sprinkle with parsley before serving.

PEANUT BUTTER—a ubiquitous paste made from macerated roasted peanuts, an invention wrongly attributed to American food scientist George Washington Carver. Peanut butter was actually invented and patented in 1884 by Montreal resident Marcellus Gilmore Edson, a full five years before Carver entered Iowa State College at Ames to study botany.

PEANUT BUTTER COOKIES—definitely of Canadian origin, since the inventor of peanut butter, Marcellus Gilmore Edson, was Canadian.

RECIPE

The Best Peanut Butter Cookies

In a bowl mix ½ cup each peanut butter, sugar, shortening and brown sugar with 1 beaten egg and 1 tsp vanilla. In another bowl mix 1½ cups flour, 1 tsp baking soda and ½ tsp salt. Add dry ingredients to wet, and mix. Roll into balls, place onto a greased cookie sheet and bake at 375° F for 10 minutes or until golden brown.

PEAR CIDER—an easy-to-make alcoholic beverage produced by fermenting pear juice in a closed container equipped with a one-way valve. No sugar or yeasts are needed, and after a few weeks of fermentation, the party can begin. Pear cider has been a Canadian treat since the 16th century and is traditionally pressed from ripe, tree-picked fruit. Pear cider is brewed by artisanal cider presses in most Canadian provinces, while the largest, Growers Cider Company in Victoria, BC, markets cider across the nation.

PEMMICAN—a high-energy food ration developed by First Nations and adopted by the earliest settlers and Hudson's Bay Company voyageurs. Meat, mostly bison, was dried and pounded almost to a flour, mixed with animal fat and berries and packed into skin bags. The HBC manufactured pemmican in Montreal and packed their product in 90-pound sacks.

P

TRIVIA

Peanuts

- Peanuts arrived in the U.S. by a circuitous route. Native to South America, peanut plants taken from Brazil to Africa by early 18th-century Portuguese traders came to North America in the pockets of slaves. Slaves planted them and ate them, and although some white farmers grew them  for pig food, the plant was mostly ignored until the Civil War, when soldiers found them a handy battlefield snack. After the war, the peanut reverted to relative obscurity until the beginning of the 20th century, when new machinery became available for harvesting. In 1901, peanut-vending machines began to pop up, and the goobers became popular at baseball games. A few years later, World War I created a huge demand for both peanuts and peanut oil. Today, the U.S. has around 1 million acres devoted to peanut cultivation, with a good percentage of that acreage becoming the Canadian invention: peanut butter.

- U.S. farmers cultivate four varieties of peanuts: runners, used mostly for peanut butter and accounting for 74 percent of production and most of Canada's imports; Virginia, used for in-shell snacking and accounting for 21 percent of production; Spanish, used for snacks, candy and some peanut butter and accounting for 4 percent of production; and Valencia, used for in-shell snacking and boiling and accounting for 1 percent of production.

- A few southern Ontario farmers grow peanuts in lieu of tobacco, but their production is one drop in a very large bucket and usually supplies value-added products such as candy or snacks sold in local retail outlets and farmland specialty stores.

- Oh, one last bit of non-essential info: the peanut is a legume, a relative of the bean, and might be considered a pea, but it is definitely no nut.

P

PEPPERMINT KNOBS CANDY—handmade in Newfoundland by Purity Factories Limited since 1924, these hard candies with the soft, chewy centres are a sweet treat no one on the east coast can live without. Purity creates other east coast necessities, such as hard biscuits or brewis, candy kisses and fruit syrups.

PERIWINKLES—introduced marine snails now common to the entire eastern seaboard. Gathered at low tide, the tasty rock crawlers are turned into soup or served up like escargots.

PEROGIES—a meat- or cheese-filled dumpling originally a culinary creation of Eastern Europeans, and brought here by immigrants at the end of the 19th century. They are naturalized into our great food experience by the addition of our Cheddar, cottage cheese, potatoes, beef, flour, mushrooms and canola oil.

PETS DE SOEUR (also called nuns' farts)—an Acadian cinnamon pastry made with leftover pie dough and still a favourite in Quebec and northern Ontario…think cinnamon roll.

P

PICKEREL. *See* walleye.

PICKLE WEED. *See* goose tongues.

PICKLED BABY CORN—a central Ontario specialty made from boiled immature field corn cobs soaked in pickling brine.

PICKLED CRABAPPLES—native crabapples boiled until soft and soaked in pickling brine syrup made by adding extra sugar to normal brine.

PICKLED EGGS—a Pennsylvania Dutch food phenomenon that arrived in Canada with the first Mennonite immigrants in the early 19th century and widely adopted as a saloon and beer parlour snack.

PIE PLANT PIE. *See* rhubarb pie.

PIGEON PIE—a common dish pre-20th century incorporating what was then the most common bird in North America, the wild pigeon.

RECIPE

Pigeon Pie

Prepare a short or puff pastry, border a baking dish and line the bottom with a slice of tender beefsteak, and season with salt, cayenne pepper and mace. Lay in as many dressed pigeons as the dish will hold after placing a pat of butter in each cavity. Season birds with salt and pepper, lay in 6 sliced, hard-boiled eggs, more butter, some veal stock or beef stock and cover with pastry. Bake at 300° F for 1½ hours.

TRIVIA

Pigeons

The wild pigeon (also called passenger pigeon) was once the most common bird in North America. A migratory bird that loved company, wild pigeon flights could number in the millions and darken the sky for hours. The commercial harvest of wild pigeons began in earnest during the early 1800s and continued until the latter part of that century, resulting in the decimation of the flocks. Hunters filled railcars, farmers blew up their roosts with black powder, and in Montreal and New York City, they sold for 2 cents each. Estimates of pigeon numbers at the turn of the 18th century run as high as five billion; two centuries later, there were none. Martha, the last of the wild pigeons, died at the Cincinnati Zoo on September 1, 1914.

PIGJEREE—a supper dish popular with west coast pioneer settlers and miners, consisting of chopped boiled bacon and rice fried until golden brown.

P

PIGWEED. *See* lamb's quarters.

PILCHARD (also called Pacific sardine)—a small, oily fish related to herrings and an important canned food item during Depression days and World War II, but now mostly used for the production of fish oil and meal. During the early 20th century, pilchard canneries dotted the west coast from California to Alaska and inspired American writer John Steinbeck to pen *Cannery Row*, a series of vignettes about life in California cannery towns during the 1930s. *See also* Atlantic herring.

PILOT BISCUITS—a brand of hard biscuit or hardtack baked by the Purity Company in Newfoundland and sold in the Far North and in some U.S. states.

PINE RIVER CHEESE—a dairymen's cheese cooperative in Ripley, Ontario, producing outstanding Cheddar cheese since 1885 and now with a brand-new facility. Pine River is a consistent prize-winner at both the British Empire Cheese Competition and the Royal Winter Fair. Product is available at over 800 retail locations in Ontario and online.

PIPSI—air-dried and smoked arctic char, a specialty of the Kivalliq region of Nunavut.

PLANKED FISH—a method of cooking fish common to west coast native peoples and best used for thicker species of fish, such as salmon and halibut. A cleaned and split fish is tacked to a cedar plank skin-side  down, brushed with oil, and the plank is then set upright next to a fire or leaned over hot coals.

RECIPE

Planked Fish

To make planked fish in a home oven, place fish fillet skin-side down on a cedar plank, brush with butter and bake at 350° F for 20–25 minutes. Make sure your plank hasn't been treated with anything or your dinner will end in disaster.

PLORINE—a French word for prostitute, which in early Quebec came to mean a mushroom cap stuffed with sausage.

PLOYE—Quebecois buckwheat pancakes cooked on one side only and used to wrap fruit or sausage.

POMME BLANCHE. See *pomme-de-prairie.*

POMME PAILLASSON—a fried potato pancake: wrap grated potatoes in a dishtowel, squeeze out water, add salt and pepper, form into pancakes and fry on both sides in butter until golden brown.

POMME-DE-PRAIRIE (*Psoralea esculenta*; also called prairie potato, breadroot, Indian breadroot, Indian turnip, prairie turnip, wild turnip, timpsula, *pomme blanche*)—a staple food of First Nations and a welcome adjunct to the diet of early settlers. Roasted or boiled, the potato-like tubers taste of slightly sweet turnip and grow from Ontario to BC. Dried, the tubers were often ground into flour by settlers and used as an ingredient in Indian meal or to extend bread flours. The tubers are still popular with foragers, and the tubers are often found for sale at farmers' markets in the Prairie Provinces. Now and then, there are attempts to cultivate the plant for commercial purposes.

POOR-MAN'S CAKE. *See* economy cake.

POOR-MAN'S PUDDING—a traditional English bread pudding popular with pioneer settlers across the nation. In the 19th

P

century, rice was substituted for bread and the dessert became synonymous with rice pudding. *See also* hard-times pudding.

POP WINE—a flavoured wine introduced in the mid-1960s that proved immensely popular. One in 20 bottles of wine sold in Canada during the 1970s was a pop variety, now called a refreshment beverage.

TRIVIA

Pop Wine

In 1952, Brights, an Ontario winemaker, introduced Winette, a sparkling emulation of a hugely popular British product called Baby Sham, a sparkling pear wine. In the mid-1960s, Andrew Peller of Andres Wines introduced the country to Cool Duck, a pop-sweet, sparkling wine made from the ubiquitous and cheap Concord and Bath grapes. Hugely successful, the foxy Cool Duck was replaced in 1971 by the astronomically successful Baby Duck, a pop-sweet sparkling wine made from a mixture of white and red Chanté grapes.

P

POPCORN—an ancient variety of Indian corn with kernels that explode and puff up when heated in oil.

PORCUPINE—any baked pudding studded with nuts that, after browning, caused the dessert to resemble a porcupine.

PORRIDGE BREAD (also called oatmeal bread)—a waste-not, want-not pioneer bread incorporating leftover porridge into the dough, but a bread that held its own and became something of an east coast favourite, even into modern times.

PORT HOPE BISCUITS—baking soda crackers that originated in the Lake Ontario region of Ontario.

PORT STANLEY ORANGEADE—called the drink that made Port Stanley famous, orangeade was the 1911 patented creation of

Mackies, a family-run beach food concession still in operation and equally famous for its French fries.

PORTULACA. *See* famine foods.

POT-EN-POT TANTE YVONNE—a lobster and fish potpie made famous by Ile de Magdalene chef Aunt Yvonne and a good enough reason to visit that island paradise.

POTATO BEAN. *See* groundnut.

POTATO BREAD—common in settler days and usually started with hop barm, this bread is still baked and enjoyed today, although the "rise" is now provided by modern yeast.

TRIVIA

Potatoes

Introduced to Europe in 1570, the Andean potato, a member of the deadly Nightshade family and considered a risky nosh by the wealthy, saw only limited cultivation by poor farmers. When French farmers enlisted to establish subsistence gardens for New World settlements in the 17th century, they took along the potato, a fortuitous inclusion for settlers of the 18th century.

P

POTATO CAKES—a culinary commonality in every pioneer kitchen and a welcome change from congealed cornmeal cakes.

RECIPE

Potato Cakes

Shred 2 potatoes and wring out well in a dish towel. Mix with 2 eggs, some salt and pepper and a little diced green onion or parsley. Form into cakes and fry until golden brown. For something a little different, add canned salmon into the preparation.

POTATO PIE—a PEI and Acadian layered casserole of thinly sliced potatoes with bacon and Cheddar cheese.

RECIPE

Potato Pie

Layer a casserole dish with bacon, followed by thinly sliced potatoes and topped with grated Cheddar cheese. Repeat the layers to the top of the dish, making sure the last layer is cheese. Bake at 375° F until bubbly and toasty brown.

TRIVIA

Potatoes

- Pioneers heading west from Montreal stocked up mainly on Indian meal (lyed corn) and pemmican, but the smart ones also took along seed potatoes, rhubarb rhizomes and various fruit and vegetable seeds to supplement those brought from home. Potatoes planted into virgin soil produced bumper crops that were often a lifesaver for destitute families. A good supply of potatoes instilled confidence in farmers and supplied their wives with yeast to make bread, starch to iron clothes and pocket warmers for milking the cow on cold mornings.

- Canadians annually consume about 75 kilograms of potatoes per person, and spuds account for around 64 percent of vegetables consumed. Total potato production is around 4.5 million tons, with the provinces of PEI, New Brunswick, Manitoba, Alberta and Ontario being the leading producers.

- Florenceville, New Brunswick, is the home of mega conglomerate McCain Foods, a company that supplies the world with over one-third of its frozen French fries. Yes, there really is a Mister Potato Head, and he lives in Florenceville, New Brunswick.

POTATO PUDDING—a waste-not, want-not dish that relieved pioneer cooks of leftover mashed potatoes. Mixed with egg, butter, sugar and nutmeg, a little leftover mashed potatoes would make a dessert, while more mashed potatoes mixed without sweetener and baked in a crust could be a dinner side for a haunch of venison.

POTATO SOUP—a mainstay meal for many early settlers in the home country, the soup took on a Canadian flavour through ingredient substitutions: venison bones instead of beef, and onions fried in that fat. In later years, the beef bone returned, but a great dollop of butter or some grated Cheddar cheese helped the soup maintain its Canadian flavour.

RECIPE

Potato Soup

Boil a shank of beef or venison and allow the broth to stand for fat skimming. Fry 4 chopped onions in the fat and add to the broth. Mash boiled potatoes and add to the broth until it reaches the consistency of heavy cream. Season with salt and pepper, top with grated Cheddar cheese and enjoy.

P

POUDING DE CHOMEUR. See hard-times pudding.

POUTINE—Acadian dumplings that evolved to become French-fried potatoes mixed with cheese curds and smothered in hot gravy or sauce. This artery-clogging Quebecois culinary invention has all manner of preparation techniques and sauce toppings.

POUTINE À TROU—an Acadian fried pie with a diced salt pork and apple filling usually topped with sugar syrup or molasses.

POUTINE

The word poutine is an Acadian borrowing of the English word pudding at a time when it meant chopped meat and spices jammed into a sock and boiled. The Acadians used the word to describe any chopped and mixed food preparation, sweet or savoury, in sock, pie or pot.

Let us fast forward to 1957, to a roadside café in Warwick, Quebec, called Café Ideal, where truck driver Eddy Lainesse sits at the counter contemplating a plate of savoury French fries. Eddy likes his French fries with ketchup but has lately found the combination boring. Eddy thinks gravy, but he hates soggy fries. Then he thinks, "If only there was something between the fries and gravy," and his eyes suddenly focus on that something.

Fernand Lachance, the proprietor of Café Ideal, sells bait boxes filled with fresh cheese curds procured from a local dairy and is busily tucking a fresh shipment into little boxes. Fernand glances over at Eddy and reads his mind. He points his cheese scoop, and says, "You want some of these curds in your fries, Eddy? You want them mixed in like—like a poutine?"

"With gravy, please," replies Eddy, smiling. The rest, as they say, is history.

POVERTY CAKE. *See* economy cake.

POWDERED MUSHROOMS. See *tabac des bois*.

PRAIRIE CHICKEN (*Tympanuchus cupido*)—a mid-sized grouse once common to Canadian prairies. Mmmm…it tastes better than chicken and is a culinary attribute much appreciated by early settlers and modern-day sportsmen, the latter appreciating the bird almost to extinction.

PRAIRIE OYSTERS—the fried testicles of male beef cattle and a culinary thrill at dude ranches and the Calgary Stampede. Beef testicles are readily available in Alberta because male beef cattle are usually castrated before reaching sexual maturity, turning them into steers.

PRAIRIE POTATO. See *pomme-de-prairie.*

PRAIRIE TURNIP. See *pomme-de-prairie.*

PRAWNS (east coast: *Pandalus borealis*, northern red prawns; west coast: *P. platyceros*, spot prawns)—both are shrimp scrumptious, especially the large west coast spot prawns when breaded with Japanese panko-style breadcrumbs and fried. East coast northern red prawns or cold water shrimps are smaller, harvested in larger quantities and are generally used in salads.

TRIVIA

Prawns

- A rose is a rose, but a prawn is a shrimp, except in Europe where it can be a langoustine or scampi. In North America, scampi are large shrimp cooked in butter and garlic, and prawns are big shrimp. Confused? You would be more so in Ireland, where prawns are still shrimp, but have tiny claws like lobsters.

- East coast shrimp fishermen catch salad shrimp for flash freezing, while west coasters haul up a variety: sidestripe, or giant shrimp, pink shrimp, prawn or spot shrimp, ocean pink shrimp and dock shrimp.

P

PROCESSED CHEESE—raised on a dairy farm in Stevensville, Ontario, J.L. Kraft saw his future in cheese. In 1903, he moved to Chicago to enter the wholesale cheese business. Struck by the waste incurred while cutting large wheels of Cheddar, he went to work on a stovetop and developed a process that incorporated wastage into a semi-solid block he called processed cheese.

PUMPKIN LOAF—ground corn and pumpkin baked in a loaf and served warm with butter and maple syrup. An 18th-century United Empire Loyalists' delight, it is still going strong today.

PUMPKIN PIE (also called squash pie)—an Acadian one-crust pie with a boiled pumpkin, egg, sugar, cream and spice filling. Perfected in the 17th century and sweetened with maple sugar, then molasses, and finally cane sugar, the pie was sometimes flavoured with brandy, a wonderful addition and a custom that survives to this day as maple and brandy pumpkin pie.

TRIVIA

Pumpkin Pie

Americans like to claim pumpkin pie as their own—part of their Pilgrim cuisine—but what the Pilgrims called pie was actually a pumpkin filled with sugar and spice and baked: what we might call pumpkin pudding. Our 17th-century Acadians loved their pies and gave us not only the pumpkin pie but also the pork pie called tourtiere.

PUMPKIN SOUP—summer in a bowl, perfected by 17th-century Acadians and enjoyed by Canadians over four centuries.

PURSLANE. *See* famine foods.

Q

QUAIL PIE—a crusted pie with the main ingredient being small game birds: bobwhite quail, snipe, woodcock, etc.

QUAKER OATS—a 1901 merger, or trust, of three oat mills spearheaded by Cleveland grain merchant Henry Crowell, owner of the Quaker Mills. The new enterprise, called the American Cereal Company, dropped a word from a Quaker Mills brand, Quaker Man, and called both their company and cereal Quaker Oats. Two years later, the Quaker Oats Company entered the Canadian market through a mill purchase in Peterborough, Ontario, and in 1912, built another in Saskatoon, Saskatchewan. Historically called the oatmeal trust, the Quaker Oats Company controlled the North American oat business from farm, to mill, to consumers. In 1983, the company bought the pork and bean company Stokely-Van Camp, makers of Gatorade, a fortuitous acquisition that enabled the conglomerate to avoid takeover overtures from mega conglomerates.

QUANANICHE—a variety of landlocked, freshwater Atlantic salmon found in various lakes in both Canada and Sweden, but the most desirable are fished from the Lake St. John area of Quebec. *See also* salmon.

QUEEN ELIZABETH CAKE (also called Queen Elizabeth squares)—a cake named after Queen Elizabeth, the late Queen Mother, and baked by Canadian women's World War II fund-raising groups. Sold by the square in munitions factories, ration queues and anywhere people gathered, the squares raised considerable monies for the war effort. The cake is delicious and easy to make. The recipe is available online.

QUEUES DE CASTORS. *See* beaver tails.

Q

R

RABBIT FRICASSEE—fried rabbit in sauce, supper for almost any backwoods traveller at any time.

> ## RECIPE
>
> ### Rabbit Fricassee
>
> *Cut a wild or domestic rabbit into 6 pieces, dredge with flour and fry. Add milk or cream, cover and cook until tender. Remove the rabbit pieces and make gravy by adding flour to the pan.*

RABBIT PIE—an every-other-night supper for early pioneer families and still a wonderful treat for modern-day culinary adventurers.

> ## RECIPE
>
> ### Rabbit Pie
>
> *Simmer a cut-up rabbit in water until tender; debone meat, season and lay aside. Fry 1 chopped onion in 3 Tbsp butter and mix in with flour to make a roux. Add rabbit meat to sauce and pour into a buttered baking dish. Cover with pastry and bake until pastry is golden.*

R

RABBIT STEW. See *bouillotte de lievre.*

RAGGED ROBINS—a favourite pioneer cookie made whenever desiccated or fresh coconut became available.

RAGOUT DE PATTES DE COCHON AVEC BOULETTES (also called meatball and pigs feet stew)—a favourite of habitants and made with beef meatballs, pigs trotters and onions, with or without vegetables.

RAILROAD CAKE—a jelly roll cake, but much lighter and named after the vehicle that brought the lightness of baking powder to farm communities—the railroad.

RECIPE

Railroad Cake

Mix 1 cup each sugar and milk, 2 cups flour, 3 beaten egg yolks, 2 tsp baking soda and 1 tsp butter. Fold in 3 whipped egg whites, pour batter into 2 shallow pans and bake immediately. While still warm, spread on jam or jelly and roll up cakes. Cool and sprinkle with powdered sugar. Makes 2 cakes.

TRIVIA

Railways

During the very early days of train travel, passengers were required to wait out the locomotive's frequent stops for fuel and water. These whistle stops would often feature a lunch counter offering sandwiches and quick meals not only to passengers but also to locals, and in many small western towns and villages they became the first restaurants.

RAINCOAST CRISP CRACKERS—small batch, all natural ingredient crackers baked by Leslie Stowe Fine Foods in Vancouver, BC, that come in five scrumptious varieties, each one a taste sensation.

RAISIN PIE—an iconic pioneer dessert pie made traditional by the Hudson's Bay Company, who insisted their outposts be stocked with various delights to reward voyageurs after a gruelling paddle. Raisin pie sweetened with real sugar in a real butter crust, along with a bottle of free rum, was every voyageur's nightly dream that came true when he reached his destination.

TRIVIA

Raisins

Raisins had been hugely popular in Europe since the time of the Romans, and in the late 17th and early 18th centuries, the dried grapes became an intrinsic commodity of the triangular trade between the Caribbean, New England and Newfoundland, and Africa. It was a foul business that enabled the slave trade, but it served to give Canadian settlers ready access to Caribbean citrus, coconut, spices, raisins and other exotic foods that came along as deck cargo on the trading ships.

R

RAMP, RAMPION. *See* wild leek.

RAPESEED OIL. *See* cold-pressed canola oil.

RAPPIE PIE (also called *pâté à la rapure*)—an Acadian boiled chicken and potato pie much favoured by both New France settlers and modern Quebecois housewives. In the early days, this dish required a long cooking time because the chicken was usually an old hen that had stopped laying eggs.

RECIPE

Rappie Pie

Dry boiled, sliced potatoes in a cloth and place in a pot with chicken stock; simmer for 10 minutes. Spread a layer of potatoes into a well-greased bake tin, add a layer of boneless chicken and another of potatoes. Top with a mixture of minced onions, chopped salt pork or bacon, season and bake for ½ hour at 350° F, or until the top is crispy brown.

RASPBERRY. See wild berries.

RED RIVER CEREAL—a breakfast porridge mix of cracked wheat, rye and flax, and a favourite of western Canadians since its 1924 introduction to the city of Winnipeg. Now manufactured by Robin Hood Multifoods, a Canadian spoke in the Smuckers food empire, the cereal is still a good-for-you start for any day and is available across the country.

RED ROCK CRAB. *See* crab.

RHUBARB PIE (also called pie plant pie)—an easy-to-make dessert pie favoured by early settlers because the rhubarb plant (*Rheum* spp.) grew fast and required little maintenance. Not a native plant, but certainly naturalized, as rhubarb crossed the country with 18th-century settlers and would always be in the ground and growing before the roof went onto cabins.

RHUBARB SAUCE—a simple pioneer dessert delicious poured over ice cream and scrumptious by itself, especially when topped with a huge dollop of whipped cream.

RECIPE

Rhubarb Sauce

Boil 4 cups cubed rhubarb in ¼ cup water with ½ cup sugar and lemon zest until rhubarb is tender, about 10 minutes. Serve as is or run through a food processor until smooth.

RICE PUDDING—a 17th-century English, baked in a sausage casing dessert naturalized to the Canadian food experience by the substitution of butter for traditional bone marrow, the addition of dried raisins or currants and the use of a pastry crust. This pudding, or pie, was a favourite with pioneers who often substituted wild rice for often hard to come by imported rice.

ROAST MOOSE—the tender loin is prime and should be hung for a minimum of two weeks, then spit-roasted over coals or a gas barbecue or oven baked.

ROAST PARTRIDGE (or roast ptarmigan)—during Canada's formative years, all small game birds (grouse, quail, snipe, etc. [*Lagopus* spp.]) common to Canada's northern areas were considered partridges and were a major food source for northern native peoples and residents of northern areas. Although there are native partridge species here, the most common in Canada, wild and farm raised, is the non-native grey, or Hungarian partridge, a member of the Pheasant family and native to Britain, not Hungary. The young birds were larded with bacon and then roasted in their own juices, one per diner.

ROAST VENISON—a saddle, or haunch, is best for roasting, cut from an animal that has been hung for a minimum of two weeks.

R

RECIPE

Roast Venison

Remove the bone and prepare a marinade of sliced onion, garlic, 1 bay leaf, 1 crushed clove and 4 juniper berries in a bottle of dry red wine or hard cider. Place meat in bowl and marinate overnight. When ready to roast, preheat oven to 450° F, tie meat into a compact shape and lard haunch with strips of bacon. Roast for 20 minutes and then reduce oven temperature to 325° F and cook for 15–20 minutes per pound.

TRIVIA

Venison

Deer were everywhere during Canada's early settlement years, and to bag the evening meal, a farmer merely had to house the dogs for the night and step from the doorway in the early morning. Not much has changed—Canadian farmers with small apple orchards can still step out the back door and bag a deer, as the delightfully agile creatures are unable to resist apple trees. They come in spring to nibble on bark and tender shoots and reappear in autumn to munch on succulent fruit. Nowadays, special fencing prevents deer from decimating large orchards, but in earlier times, only man's best friend enabled evolution of the legendary Canadian apple pie.

ROAST WILD DUCK—around a quarter of a million wild ducks are harvested annually in Canada, and roasting is the preferred method of preparation.

RECIPE

Roast Duck

Clean and stuff the birds with your favourite bread stuffing and pop them into a preheated, 400° F oven until they brown, then reduce heat to 250° F and bake for 2–2½ hours, until tender. To make gravy, deglaze the pan with water or wine, thicken with flour and season with salt and pepper. Roast wild ducks with gravy...
scrumptious.

ROAST WILD GOOSE—while modern consumers shudder at the thought of digging into what have become feathered rats in most areas, our pioneer forefathers had no such aversion. Oiled, seasoned and roasted as for a regular recipe, Canada geese harvested from the wild are a mighty tasty treat, especially larded over with strips of bacon. In the early days, Canada geese suffered the fate of bison and were nearly hunted to extinction, but thanks to conservation efforts have made a spectacular comeback. Snow geese are a species hunted in the Far North and some east coast areas, while in the old days several species of swans were pioneer fare.

ROASTED PIG TAILS—a Waterloo County, Ontario, specialty. Real tails from real pigs and very yummy, but watch your teeth, as they can break easily while munching on pig tail.

ROASTED ROUNDER—an immature codfish roasted whole; a Newfoundland favourite dinner fish.

ROBIN HOOD FLOUR—a favourite of Canadian bakers since 1909, when Minneapolis grain miller F.A. Bean refurbished an old

R

mill in Moose Jaw, Saskatchewan, and began producing quality wheat flour with the familiar red and green Robin Hood logo.

ROCK GUTS. *See* famine foods.

ROCK SAMPHIRE (*Crithmum maritimum*; also called sea asparagus)—an edible plant found along coastal areas of Europe and North America and a favourite vegetable of coastal First Nations. Adopted by early settlers and still popular, the plant has a pleasant, hot and spicy taste that is perfect for green salads or pickling.

ROCK TRIPE (*Umbilicaria vellea*; also called *tripe de roche*)—rock lichen gathered by voyageurs to bolster pemmican stew. It isn't very tasty, but it was always underfoot and ready for picking.

ROOT BEER—spruce beer, with sugar, spices, herbs and vanilla replacing the pungent spruce tips. Canadian settlers were drinking various root beers long before Pennsylvania pharmacist and vanilla broker Charles E. Hires decided to add a little vanilla, sarsaparilla, ginger and sassafras. He patented his recipe and made millions, much of that lucre coming from Canada, as his original bottled extract became a huge hit with Maritimers.

R

ROSE HIP JELLY—a pioneer settler's favourite right across the nation; rose hips are easily gathered, and the jelly is easy to make and a preferred glaze for venison.

ROSE WATER—perfumed water prepared by steeping or distilling rose petals and used as a cooking ingredient, room freshener and cosmetic. Roses grow everywhere in Canada, and while distilling the essence from the fragrant flower sounds daunting and beyond the capabilities of both early settlers and contemporary citizens, it is a rather simple undertaking.

WILD ROSE HIPS

The wild rose bush was ubiquitous in Canada, and First Nations used the hips, or fruit of the bush, to make a tea, probably suspecting the hips were loaded with something that provided a health benefit (vitamin C). Rose hips are picked after a touch of frost has turned them a reddish colour, when they look like cherry-sized apples—an attribute they come by honestly, as the two are related. Tart and tangy, the hips are nicely tamed by sugar and are best used for jelly making because the straining rids the mixture of a million seeds.

RECIPE

Rose Water

Place an inverted bowl at the bottom of a large stockpot and surround with rose petals. Place another bowl right side up on top of the inverted bowl and fill pot with water to cover petals. Place lid on stockpot upside down (concave top is best), pile chipped or cubed ice on the inverted top and begin the cooking process. Steam containing aromatic rose essence will condense on the stockpot lid and drip down into the catch bowl. This process will yield around 2 cups of rose water that should be bottled and capped to prevent evaporation. Use in recipes that call for rose water, or use to make cold cream. Pioneer women heated beechnut oil with beeswax and, while stirring constantly, dribbled in as much rose water as the emulsion could carry.

R

RUBBABOO—a trapper's stew or porridge made from anything on hand: pemmican, a bit of last week's venison, a few handfuls of Indian meal and whatever could be picked off along the trail. The name is derived from burgoo, a British navy slang word for oatmeal gruel served up on 18th-century ships of the line.

RUCKLE BEANS—similar to lima beans, and while they are not native to BC's Salt Spring Island, it is the only place on the planet that they are grown commercially. Brought to Salt Spring by Ontario farmer Henry Ruckle, the beans have been part of the Ruckle family for over a century. What happened to the beans' Ontario progenitors is a mystery—not a trace survives. Their demise in Ontario could have had something to do with their tendency to turn into soup if over-boiled, but the folks on Salt Spring Island prefer them baked, so the Ruckle bean's survival is pretty much guaranteed.

RUM—the distilled fermentation of boiled sugar, or molasses, and along with fish, furs and timber, an economic engine that drove our nation to Confederation. During the 18th and 19th centuries, every British sailor and soldier got a pint a day, fishermen got double or triple that, and every man, woman or child with a penny could buy a pint. Rum paid for our fish that fed slaves in the Caribbean, and rum bought the slaves to cut more Caribbean cane to make more rum to buy more cod. Round and around it went, while the trading company owners got filthy rich. It was a nasty business, but then so was killing millions of beaver and buffalo, and cutting down all the trees.

RUM BALLS—originally a sailor's dessert made by soaking hardtack in rum and molasses, but later made respectable by the substitution of graham crackers, cocoa and corn syrup.

RUM SHRUB—in the 17th, 18th and 19th centuries, rum was usually distilled badly and vile tasting. With some added sugar and citrus juice, the worst-tasting rum could be made into a palatable cocktail called shrub, the father of all cocktails, and

R

probably called that because of the many imbibers who woke up under the shrubbery. *See also* shrub.

RYE WHISKY—in our nation's formative years, most whisky was distilled from either 100 percent or a good portion of fermented rye grain, hence the name rye whisky. Then along came cheaper grains, like corn and wheat, and rye slipped to a small percentage. However, for the aficionado of real Canadian whisky, Alberta Springs in Calgary, Alberta, is still in the straight rye whisky business. Try their reserve whiskies and be ready for a lip-smacking experience.

TRIVIA

Whisky

- By 1840, well over 200 whisky distillers operated in Canada, most producing a product distilled from rye grain mash. Most of those distillers started out as millers, grinding grain into flour, and the traditional payment was 10 percent of the grain: the grain tithe. Over time, as farmers increased yields of grain, the tithe began to pile up and become a problem for millers. The solution was to turn it into whisky.

- During Prohibition, Canada stopped short of banning the production and export of whisky. Cuba and Mexico became the main destinations for Canadian whisky, but few ships ever got farther than the U.S., and since Prohibition was unpopular legislation in the U.S., law enforcement generally turned a blind eye. Canadian distillers worked 24/7 to meet U.S. demand; grain farmers and fast boatbuilders prospered; and fishermen on both coasts and the Great Lakes made fortunes transporting fish of a different colour. Distillers even packed bottles in burlap bags to make drops and pickups at sea easier.

- In Canada, unlike the U.S. or Britain where whisky is spelled with an "e," as in Scotch whiskey or Bourbon whiskey, our word is spelled with no "e": whisky.

R

S

SAGAMITE—a First Nations corn soup made not from kernels or cobs but from ground corn flour, and widely adopted by pioneer settlers.

SALAD BURNET (*Poterium sanguisorba*)— a perennial member of the Rose family with leaves tasting like cucumber. Foraged by native peoples and cultivated by settlers, this herb has become popular with upscale chefs. It is used in a variety of ways, but mostly for salad greens.

SALALBERRY JAM—a tart, wintergreen-flavoured jam made from berries of the Pacific coast salal shrub (*Gaultheria shallon*), an evergreen member of the Wintergreen family and an important food source for coastal First Nations. Salalberries were gathered and dried in blocks for winter food, with a portion pounded into jam used to cut the grease of roasted game. Salalberries look and taste a bit like blueberries and are so rich in pectin that they turn to jam when macerated, and no additional pectin is required to make jelly. Salal shrubs grow everywhere along the coast and can be identified by their dark green, waxy leaves.

SALMON—common name for species of the Salmonidae family of fish, including trout; an important historical and modern-day food and income source for many Canadians.

SALMON

Atlantic salmon (*Salmo salar*; also called spring salmon, quananiche, silver salmon, grayling, bay salmon) is a mostly anadromous species, meaning it spawns in fresh water, moves into the sea and returns to fresh water to spawn. Atlantic salmon may also be landlocked, much to the delight of early pioneers who found the Great Lakes teeming with the fish. However, by the late 1800s, that teeming had become nothing owing to overfishing and habitat loss, unfortunate calamities that also occurred on our east coast, where commercial fishing has been supplanted by aquaculture. Unlike Pacific salmon, the Atlantic variety is iteroparous, meaning it does not die after spawning and may live up to 20 years. Atlantic salmon is the preferred species of east coast fish smokers, and while most of their fish is farm raised, a few have access to wild fish. Either way, they smoke up one delicious product.

Pacific salmon (*Oncorhynchus nerka*) is an anadromous species that includes many genera and trout, of which only the salmon are semelparous, meaning they die after spawning. While Pacific salmon species are under constant threat from overfishing, habitat destruction and pollution, their numbers are still high when compared to the Atlantic variety, and in some cases, populations are rebounding owing to remedial action by authorities. The most important commercial salmon varieties are sockeye, coho, chinook, chum and pink salmon.

S

TRIVIA

Salmon

- The natural pink or reddish colour of salmon flesh is because the fish consume krill or shellfish that contain carateniods. Farm-raised salmon fed a plant- or wild fish–based diet have little colour and no marketability, so artificial dyes are added to their food.

- It takes almost 4 kilograms of wild caught fish to produce 1 kilogram of farmed salmon.

- Ninety-nine percent of Atlantic salmon for retail sale are farmed, while only 20 percent of Pacific salmon are the product of aquaculture, with most canned salmon being from the wild.

- Salmon are vulnerable to a parasitic nematode called *Anisakis*. If ingested from raw salmon by humans, it causes a debilitating disease called *Anisakiasis*—it is best not to consume raw salmon.

SALMON BURGERS—a salmon patty popularized by upscale British Columbia restaurants and TV chefs. Not a fish cake, the salmon burger patty is constructed differently.

RECIPE

Salmon Burgers

Place 1–1½ lbs half-frozen salmon fillets in a food processor and pulse to a mince. Transfer to a bowl and combine with 1 egg, 2 tsp fresh dill, 1 Tbsp sour cream, ½ cup cornmeal, 1 tsp sea salt and ¼ cup canola oil. Form patties, fry gently until brown, and serve on a soft roll.

SALMON JERKY—traditionally made by deep slicing salmon fillets, curing with maple or camas sugar and smoking over an alder fire for days. Nowadays, fillets are skinned, sliced and cured with brown sugar, smoked for a day, thin sliced and smoked again. It's still a tasty product, but not as good as the old days.

SALMON LOAF—popular during war and economic depression, and with moms in a dither, the salmon loaf has endeared itself to generations of Canadians. Originally made with fresh fish and confined to coastal area kitchens, the loaf spread like flu when cheap canned salmon flooded into markets toward the end of the 19th century.

RECIPE

Salmon Loaf

Combine 1 can drained salmon, 1 cup breadcrumbs, ¾ cup milk, 1 egg slightly beaten, ¼ cup minced onion and 2 Tbsp melted butter. Season with salt and pepper, fluff with a fork, transfer to a bread tin, pat into a loaf shape and bake at 350° F for 50–60 minutes.

TRIVIA

Canned Salmon

British Columbia's salmon industry began in 1824, when the Hudson's Bay Company post at Langley began purchasing salmon from native peoples and salt curing it in barrels. By 1834, the HBC was packing and shipping 3000 to 4000 barrels annually. Then in 1870, Alexander Loggie, who had learned the canning process in his native New Brunswick, convinced a few other gentlemen to join him in a canning venture. Canned salmon took off like a rocket, and in a few years, the company was packing and shipping 100,000 cases per year. By the turn of the century, dozens of canneries were established and packing almost 2 million cases per year.

S

SALMON PATTIES—canned salmon combined with egg, breadcrumbs, minced onion and seasonings. Patty cake, patty cake, roll them in flour, refrigerate for an hour and fry.

SALMONBERRY JAM—an easy to make jam from the drupes, or berries, of the salmonberry bush (*Rubus spectabilis*), a member of the mighty Rose family. Salmonberries look like and have a taste similar to their raspberry relatives and can be foraged all over the Pacific Northwest. When foraging salmonberries, keep in mind that the yellowish berries are sweetest.

SALSIFY (*Tragopogon porrifolius*; also called oyster plant)— a root vegetable popular with Canadians until the root cellar was made redundant by the introduction of refrigeration. Brought along with other root vegetables in the early 18th century, salsify took to Canadian gardens like a native plant, surpassing its European parentage in both size and taste. Also called oyster plant because the taste is best described as a cross between oysters and asparagus, the salsify root has become a naturalized Canadian vegetable. Salsify roots resemble parsnips or carrots, and its grass-like leaves make good salad greens when cut and allowed to grow back as tender shoots. Salsify has lately become a favourite with upscale chefs and is once again being cultivated, albeit in small quantities.

SALT COD—a codfish cleaned, split, rubbed with salt, washed and dried in the sunshine until dehydrated. The process was discovered by 16th-century Basque fishermen plying the coastal waters of Newfoundland.

SALT COD CASSEROLE—an east coast favourite then and now, the dish is a simple preparation of cooked rice with an overlay of flaked cod, overlaid with a mix of chopped onions, green peppers and tomatoes, followed by another layer of rice, a drenching with white sauce and a half-hour bake in a moderate oven.

S

SALT COD

To prepare salt cod for cooking, cover it with cold water and soak for 48 hours, changing the water six or seven times. If time is a factor, soak overnight, drain and simmer 15 minutes—if it's still too salty, cover with water and simmer again.

TRIVIA

Salt Cod

- Before the Basque discovery of salting, codfish were simply dried in the air, making the flesh difficult to keep and unappetizing. The salt, brought as ship ballast, enabled a longer shelf life and an extremely palatable product.

- The process of salting began with the unloading of codfish at the stage (the cleaning dock). On the stage, the fish were gutted, headed, split, washed and taken to the salting compound, where they were left to cure for a number of weeks. Cured, the fish were washed free of salt and taken to the raised drying platforms, called flakes. Drying, or making, fish was difficult, backbreaking work, as every storm required that the fish be gathered and redistributed after the weather cleared. At season's end, the salt cod was packed aboard a ship and sent to salt fish buyers in Europe in exchange for goods, a trust-in-God endeavour called "the voyage" because the ships would often run into foul weather and sink.

S

SALT HERRING. *See* Digby chicken.

SALT RISING BREAD—the no-yeast bread leavening method used by early pioneer settlers.

RECIPE

Salt Rising Bread

Mix 1 cup each cornmeal and water, pour into 1 pint boiling water, stir constantly for 5 minutes and set off the heat. Add 2 pints fresh milk still warm from the cow and 1 Tbsp each sugar and salt. Let cool, stir in enough flour to make a batter and keep in a warm place for 4 hours. Add 1 pint buttermilk, 1 tsp baking soda and enough flour to make a soft dough. Mould onto a greased pan, let rise for 1 hour and bake.

SALT SPRING ISLAND CHEESES—superlative sheep, goat and cows' milk cheeses made by artisan cheese makers using some of the finest milk on the planet. Salt Spring Island Cheese Company makes delectable goat and sheep's milk cheeses, while the ladies at Moonstruck produce a variety of marvellous cheeses with milk from their all-Jersey herd.

TRIVIA

Salt Spring Island

Salt Spring Island is the largest and most populated of the Southern Gulf Islands and is located between Vancouver Island and the mainland in the Straight of Georgia.

S

SALT SPRING ISLAND LAMB—the world's finest lamb. Salt air, lush forage and a temperate climate all contribute to produce a succulent, flavourful meat that is beyond compare.

> ### TRIVIA
>
> **Lamb**
>
> Sheep destined for the dinner plate are graded according to age: baby lamb is 6–8 weeks old, spring lamb is 3–5 months, lamb is 5–12 months and yearling lamb is 1–2 years, while mutton is anything over 2 years.

SALTED CAPLIN. *See* capelin.

SAND BAKED BEANS—dried beans or peas are soaked in water to soften, then seasoned, sweetened and placed into a sealed bean pot and buried under a pile of super heated campfire rocks to cook.

SANDFIRE GREENS. *See* goose tongues.

SARDINE. *See* Atlantic herring. *See also* Pacific herring.

SASKATOON (*Amelanchier alnifolia*; also called serviceberry)—a member of the Rose family growing profusely from western Ontario to BC. Similar in colour and shape to blueberries, the purple-coloured saskatoon berries have a unique taste. They are easily gathered and made into marvellous jams, jellies, pies and puddings.

> ### TRIVIA
>
> **Saskatoon Berries**
>
> The Saskatchewan city of Saskatoon derives its name from the saskatoon berry, while the word saskatoon itself is the anglicized Cree word for the berry, *mis-sask-quah-toomina*.

S

SASKATOON BERRIES

Saskatoons were dietary lifesavers for early voyageurs and trappers. The berry was a main constituent of pemmican, that easily carried and nutritious pounded meat ration produced by First Nations. Prairie settlers also relied on the berries, and for many of them, saskatoons were the only fresh fruit available. Gathered in large quantities, the berries were prepared using a method perfected by First Nations: clean the berries, boil them down to a sludge, pour into bread tins and dry in the sunshine like bricks. Berry bricks featured large in prairie cuisine, as chips from the brick flavoured stews, coated roasted game and made wonderful dessert creations. Nowadays, the berries are both foraged from the wild and cultivated. They are gaining popularity for their antioxidant, cancer-preventing qualities. Looks like a blueberry, tastes like a blueberry, it is actually a super fruit in disguise, as the saskatoon berry is packed full of nutritional qualities not found in blueberries.

S

SASKATOON PIE (also called serviceberry pie)—the iconic berry pie of Canada's Prairie Provinces and often combined with rhubarb to make another favourite, saskatoon rhubarb pie.

SCOFF. *See* jiggs dinner.

SCREECH—rum once distilled in Newfoundland from the dregs that accumulated at the bottom of molasses barrels. Screech is still popular in Newfoundland, but it is now made and bottled in the Caribbean and distributed by the brand owner, the Newfoundland Liquor Commission.

SCRUNCHIONS—cubed salt pork or fatback bacon fried crispy and used as topping for brewis and dozens of other east coast specialty foods. Salt pork fried without cubing is called vang.

SEA ASPARAGUS (*Salicornia virginici*)—a marine plant harvested annually along the BC coast and Vancouver Island. Sea asparagus resembles regular asparagus but has a salty, fresh taste of the sea that goes well with fish. Sea asparagus is shipped out frozen and is available online from several BC packers. *See also* rock samphire.

SEA PARSLEY (*Palmaria palmata*; also called Nova Scotia sea parsley)—a natural mutation of dulse discovered by National Research Council of Canada scientists in 1978 and licensed to a Nova Scotia company, Ocean Produce International, for production by aquaculture. A unique Canadian product, as it exists only in OPI's aquaculture tanks, sea parsley's burgundy-coloured florets run a gamut of tastes from celery to bacon to mussels to smoked oysters. It is available fresh, sun dried or oven toasted.

SEA PIE. See *cipaille.*

SEA URCHIN ROE (also called umi)—roe from green sea urchins (*Strongylocentrotus droebachiensis*) is consumed from the spiny bottom dwellers using a spoon, cooked by upscale chefs, or made into sushi, when it is called umi. Green sea urchins are found on both coasts, mostly off of BC and New Brunswick. Another, the red urchin (*S. franciscanus*), is only in the Pacific, with both harvested solely by scuba divers.

S

SEAFOOD CHOWDER—the Mi'kmaq would have plied the earliest French explorers with chowder while trying to part them from their iron, cloth and rope. If those explorers were around today, they would instantly recognize chowder, as the basic recipe has changed little. The Mi'kmaq would have used seal oil for butter, wild leeks for onions, boiled hickory nuts for potatoes and wild mustard for spice, while the fish would have been lobster, cod, haddock, oysters and clams. There would have been no cream in it, but nowadays it's called Manhattan-style chowder.

SEAL FLIPPER PIE—despite the name, this east coast favourite contains not a shred of seal flipper. The word flipper refers to the front shoulder meat of seals, corresponding to a shoulder of lamb or pork, while the actual flippers are paws, the front called fippers and the rear, daddles.

RECIPE

Seal Flipper Pie

Soak flipper meat in cold water and baking soda for an hour or so to dissipate any fishy taste, then remove the fat, cube the meat, dredge it in flour and brown it in a hot pan with onions and bacon. Cover the pan and bake for 2–3 hours. When done, top the pie with pastry and bake for another 20 minutes to brown the crust.

SEAL FLIPPERS

Seal flippers are an early spring tradition in Newfoundland that residents are more than happy to keep secret. If the rest of Canada knew what taste treats that tradition yielded up, the path to the big island would be deep and wide. April is when the sealing boats return to port, and residents must be quick to the docks because seal flippers sell out quickly. Properly prepared, seal flipper is fork tender and one of the tastiest meats on the planet.

SEAWEED SALAD—a popular BC salad made with sliced tomatoes, cucumber and greens harvested from the ocean. Among the favourite seaweed greens are winged kelp, feather boa, nori, rockweed, sea cabbage, sea lettuce and rainbow seaweed. Sun dried, these seaweed varieties are available across Canada in specialty food stores or online.

SERVICEBERRY. *See* saskatoon.

SERVICEBERRY PIE. *See* saskatoon pie.

SHAD (*Alosa sapidissima*; also called American shad)—the largest member of the Herring family, averaging about 2 kilograms, and a historically important east coast source of food and revenue. Shad are anadromous, meaning they live in the sea and spawn in fresh water, and for shad that is usually rivers in early spring, a few weeks after the alewife run. During the 1800s, up to 50 million tons of shad were caught annually and consumed fresh, pickled or smoked. Nowadays, with numbers drastically reduced by overfishing and habitat destruction, only small commercial fisheries still exist, with fish caught mainly for roe. In our Maritime Provinces, the appearance of shad roe in fish markets is an anticipated culinary event and a sure sign that spring has arrived. Introduced into Pacific waters in 1871, shad have become established from Alaska to California but are not sought by commercial fishermen there.

SHEE FISH. *See* inconnu.

SHEEP SORREL (*Rumex acetosella*)—brought and planted by early pioneer settlers, sheep sorrel has a delightful lemony flavour and is used to make marvellous soups, salads, jams and pies. Not happy to remain in gardens, the plant escaped into the wild and became an invasive weed. Sheep sorrel is a small commercial crop in Canada, but it is widely foraged and usually found at farmers' markets.

SHEEPBERRIES. *See* nannyberries.

S

SHEPHERD'S PIE. See *pâté chinois.*

SHIPWRECK CASSEROLE—a layered, one-dish casserole with east coast roots, but popular across Canada.

RECIPE

Shipwreck Casserole

Mix 1 can tomato soup with 1 can corn and pour half over a layer of potatoes, onions and rice. Layer with peas, ground beef or sausage and add remaining corn and soup mix. Bake at 350° F for 1½ hours, top with cheese and bacon, and brown for 15 minutes.

SHIRRIFF GOOD MORNING MARMALADE—a uniquely Canadian breakfast delight from one of the greatest family-run food businesses in Canada. Now owned by Smuckers, along with most other iconic Canadian brands, Shirriff is still producing fine marmalades with that unique flavour Canadians love, a rare occurrence in the grab-bag world of buying and selling our heritage branded foods.

SHISHAMO. *See* capelin.

SHRIMP—our main commercially caught shrimp is *Pandalus borealis*, or pink shrimp. They are smaller than tropical varieties but have sweeter meat and are great for salads and cocktails and as an accompaniment for fish dishes. Since all Canadian shrimp are harvested from the wilds, a "Product of Canada" designation means the frozen shrimp you purchase were not raised in a ditch. Pink shrimp are caught in both Atlantic and Pacific oceans, but the main harvest is concentrated in the Atlantic.

SHRUB—a sugar-sweetened brandy, wine and spice punch of English origin, but naturalized through the substitution of backyard whisky or rum, applejack and maple sugar. The father of all cocktails, shrub was probably called so because after a few too many, that is where imbibers would wake up: under a shrub. A favourite of pioneer men, barrels of shrub were stored away in barns and root cellars, providing settlers a welcome respite from hard times...hic!

SILKY SWALLOW WORT. *See* milkweed.

SILVER SALMON. *See* salmon.

SINGLE MALT WHISKY—a Scottish-style Highland whisky distilled on Cape Breton by Glenora Distillery, the only distillery operation of its kind in North America.

SISCOWET—a rotund, very oily variety of lake trout caught only in the deepest sections of Lake Superior and smoked like herring.

SLUMGULLION—an east coast fishermen's stew made from fish scraps, usually cod.

SMALLAGE. *See* Indian celery.

SMELT (Osmeridae family)—a small, iridescent fish closely related to salmon that reproduces in prodigious numbers in both salt and fresh water.

SMOKED FISH—whitefish, salmon, herring, halibut, black cod, sturgeon, char, eel, mackerel, trout and just about any fish hauled from our oceans, lakes and rivers can be smoked hot, cool, brined or sugared. One of the biggest and best commercial fish smokers is a company aptly named Grizzly in Saint-Agustin, near Quebec City. Grizzly smokes wild and farmed salmon, halibut and trout by the cold smoke method and has recently added a hot smoke facility to process other fish varieties, including sturgeon. Grizzly smoked fish is available at supermarkets and specialty food shops nationwide.

SMOKED PORK JOWLS. See *oreilles de crisse*.

S'MORES—a campfire treat of roasted marshmallow and melted chocolate sandwiched between two graham crackers.

S

While Americans like to think of this creation as theirs, anyone who has attended a Canadian summer camp knows the true origin of the gooey delight.

SNIPE IN SAUCE—a meal prepared by our pioneer settler ancestors.

RECIPE

Snipe in Sauce

Melt ½ lb butter in a frying pan, then add 6 cleaned snipe, breasts down. Add 1 Tbsp each chopped wild onion (ramp) and dried apples. Cook for 7–10 minutes, remove birds, deglaze pan with apple cider and use for a sauce.

SNIPE PIE—any crusted pie using small birds as the main ingredient. During our formative years, hunters firing gravel shot considered any flock of small birds fair game. Shore birds, migratory birds, blackbirds, songbirds, it mattered little; stripped of feathers, they all looked and tasted pretty much the same.

SNOW TAFFY. *See* maple taffy.

SNOWBALLS—a product of the English candy maker Lee's, the Lee's Snowball has been a favourite Maritime sweet for generations; however, if Maritimers cannot get a Lee's fix, they will make their own snowballs.

S

RECIPE

Snowballs

Boil 3 cups sugar, ¾ cup butter and 1¼ cups milk to a temperature of 230° F. In a bowl, combine 3 cups rolled oats, 1 cup unsweetened coconut and ¾ cup cocoa powder, and mix well with liquid. Cool and form into balls, roll in additional coconut and chill.

SNOWBERRY. *See* capillaire.

SOAPBERRY JAM. *See* buffaloberry jam.

SOLOMON GUNDY—pirate food, originally called salmagundi and brought to the east coast by those brigands of the high seas, the Caribbean buccaneers. The dish became solomon gundy because of Newfoundland dialect and changed from a catchall ingredient cold stew into a herring pickle.

RECIPE

Solomon Gundy

Clean 6 herring, cut into 1 inch pieces and soak in water 24 hours. Squeeze water from herring and place into a Mason jar with sliced onion in alternating layers. In a saucepan, heat 2 cups vinegar. Add ½ cup sugar and 2 Tbsp pickling spice. Let vinegar mixture cool, pour over fish and onions and store jars in a cool spot. Best served with sour cream and extra fresh onions.

SOOPOLALLIE JAM. *See* buffaloberry jam.

SORTILEGE—a blended in Quebec Canadian whisky and maple syrup liqueur popular with upscale chefs and mixologists.

SOURDOUGH BISCUITS—bread rolls risen with an adapted yeast starter, a combination of wild and domestic yeasts. Made with flour, water and yeast, the starter has a sour milk smell, hence the name. Sourdough is a word synonymous with old-time, northern miners and pioneer settlers who used the starter. During the late 1960s, sourdough starter was rediscovered by adventurous bakers and has become immensely popular nationwide.

S

RECIPE

Sourdough Starter

Boil 2 large peeled potatoes until they fall apart. Place potatoes into a non-metallic bowl and mash while slowly adding 2 cups water. Beat mixture while adding in 1⅔ cups unbleached flour, 3 Tbsp salt and ½ tsp active  *dried yeast. Set aside 24 hours for starter to acquire its characteristic sour taste. To keep starter alive, feed every other day with ¼ cup water and ½ cup flour.*

SOUSED MACKEREL—an east coast pickled fish favourite, wherein mackerel fillets are cooked boiled in vinegar, water and pickling spice, and served cooled on ice or at room temperature.

SOYBEANS—roasted as a snack food, ground into flour for bread-making or made into tofu, soybeans have made inroads into the Canadian food experience through efforts of the Harrow Research Centre in Harrow, Ontario. Harrow has been so successful in producing soybean varieties that Japanese buyers have dubbed their latest release Harowvintin, the Asian pearl. Veggie burgers and other food products made from soy are available at supermarkets everywhere.

SPICE CAKE—a molasses spice cake popular with Maritimers. Salt cod traded for West Indies molasses, ginger and spices provided early access to ingredients that became pervasive in east coast cuisine.

SPLAKE—a hybrid fish; a cross between lake and brook trout first developed in western Canada around 1946, but a breeding program was not earnestly undertaken until the late 1950s, when the federal Department of Lands and Forests began to rehabilitate the collapsed lake trout fishery in the Great Lakes. A wonderful game fish, the splake is also one of the best-tasting fish and is much used by upscale restaurant chefs.

SPOT PRAWNS. *See* prawns.

SPOTTY DOG—a fruit-and-suet pudding and an east coast take on the English favourite, spotted dick. Maritimers usually added local berries to replace the chopped dates and figs called for in the traditional spotted dick recipe.

SPRAT. *See* Atlantic herring.

SPRING HERRING. *See* alewife.

SPRING SALMON. *See* salmon.

SPRUCE BEER—an alcoholic adaptation of a piney decoction brewed by First Nations before the arrival of Europeans. Introduced to Jacques Cartier during his second voyage to New France by members of the Iroquois nation, the nonalcoholic version of the brew cured Cartier's men of the dreaded scurvy. From that date on, spruce beer became a medicinal tonic for voyageurs, fur trappers and settlers, who quickly found that fermentation made the brew slightly more palatable.

RECIPE

Spruce Beer

Pound tender shoots of the black spruce tree to a resinous essence until you have 8 oz. Take 4 oz hops and boil ½ hour in 1 gallon water. Strain and add 16 gallons warm water, 2 gallons molasses and the spruce essence dissolved in 1 quart water. Pour into a clean cask, shake well, add ½ pint cider dregs and let stand for 1 week. When drawn off, add 1 Tbsp molasses per bottle.

S

SPRUCE GUM—the favourite chewing gum of First Nations and quickly adopted by pioneer settlers. Spruce resin is gathered, aged three to four days, and popped into the mouth for a good chew. The Cree people not only chewed the gum, but also used it to extract sharp, pointed wild rice kernels from their eyes during the harvest. In Newfoundland, spruce resin gum collected for chewing is called frankum.

SPRUCE TEA—a tea made by infusing the tender tips of white spruce, black spruce, hemlock or cedar in hot water.

TRIVIA

Spruce

A native cedar credited with saving Jacques Cartier and crew from a grisly death by scurvy during their 1535 exploration of the St. Lawrence River is named for that occasion and called *Arbor Vitae*—now arborvitae—the tree of life.

SQUASH CASSEROLE—a First Nations dish adapted to the tastes of early settlers by the addition of applesauce, egg, butter and seasoning to cooked and puréed squash.

SQUASH PIE. *See* pumpkin pie.

SQUASHBERRY. *See* partridgeberry.

SQUASHBERRY PUDDING. *See* partridgeberry pudding.

SQUASHBERRY WINE (also called partridgeberry wine, foxberry wine, squatum)—a Newfoundland alcoholic beverage made from partridgeberries, a close relative of the cranberry. Newfoundlanders called them squashberries because they needed a good squashing to promote fermentation and make the wine most commonly called squatum.

S

SQUASH

Native to South America, the squash plant migrated north as a constituent of the "three sisters," corn, beans and squash, the traditional planting method of First Nations cultivators. Beans supply nutrients to the corn, and big-leaved squash plants shade tender corn shoots and conserve water. When the Europeans arrived  in North America, they found many varieties of squash readily available. Boiled, mashed squash aside a haunch of venison would have graced many a pioneer table.

SQUATUM. *See* squashberry wine.

ST. ALBERT CHEESE—a dairymen's cheese cooperative in St. Albert, Ontario, producing outstanding Cheddar cheese since 1894. St. Albert cheese is a consistent prize-winner at both the British Empire Cheese Competition and the Royal Winter Fair. The product is available at many Ontario and Quebec retail locations and online.

STARFLOWER. *See* borage.

STE-CATHERINE'S TAFFY—a pulled taffy candy traditionally made by Quebec children to celebrate Ste-Catherine's Day.

STE-JULIE CREAM FUDGE—the best fudge in the world and a true Canadian success story that began in 1979, when Francine Nantel sold her first batch from her husband's convenience store. Francine's fudge had a "wow" factor, and the public was soon clamouring for so much more that the couple opened a small plant in Ste-Julie, Quebec. Over the years, the plant grew larger and the fudge flavours more numerous, but the Nantel family still holds to old-fashioned values and has preserved the "wow."

STENCHEL (also called switchel)—a cheap Maritime drink made to quench the thirst of farm labourers. It is a mixture of molasses, vinegar and ginger stirred into cold water.

ST-HUBERT—a Quebec restaurant chain serving rotisserie chicken along with the best gravy on the planet. In Quebec, St-Hubert is comfort food *par excellance*, and the company, Rotisseries St-Hubert, is in the top 10 of *Commerce Magazine*'s most admired Quebec companies.

STOVIES—a Scottish one-pot dish made Canadian by the use of wild game, especially buffalo.

> ## RECIPE
>
> ### Stovies
>
> *Melt 2 Tbsp drippings in a large cooking pot and soften 2 sliced onions. Add ½ lb cubed buffalo meat, season, layer on 2 lbs sliced potatoes, and pour on 12 oz stock. Bake for 1 hour, or until liquid is absorbed and potatoes brown.*

S

STRAWBERRIES. *See* wild berries.

STRAWBERRY JAM—Canada's favourite breakfast jam since 1534, when Jacques Cartier found strawberries of excellent size and taste growing everywhere in New France.

STUFFED MEATLOAF—a Depression days or ration extending meal popular right across the country. It's simple to make: line the bottom and sides of a bread tin with ground meat prepared for meatloaf, stuff the middle with bread dressing and bake for 1½ hours.

STURGEON *À LA* STE-MENEHOULD—a wine-poached sturgeon fillet served in a Ste-Menehould sauce, a creamy concoction named for the patron saint of the French town that originated the sauce. During the 17th and early 18th centuries, sturgeon from the St. Lawrence River near Quebec City were cleaned, salted and packed into barrels and used as a primary winter food item. The fish also yielded caviar, a much-appreciated luxury during the hard early days.

SUCCOTASH—an original First Nations dish of cooked beans and corn, but adapted to European settlers' tastes by the addition of butter, seasoning, a scrape or two of nutmeg and a bit of salt pork. Many variations exist, with many types of beans used and with tomatoes sometimes added.

SUCRE À LA CRÈME—a traditional Quebecois cream fudge.

SUMAC TEA (also called fragrant sumac tea)—an excellent tea made by soaking the ripe, red fruit of the sumac tree (*Rhus aromatica*) in hot, not boiling, water for 15 minutes and then reheating the infusion. Surprisingly refreshing, it is very tasty and needs no sweetening. It's also delicious served cold as a summer beverage, with a taste reminiscent of lemonade.

S

SUNCHOKE. *See* Jerusalem artichoke.

SUNFLOWER SOUP—a First Nations sunflower and game meat soup widely adopted by settlers and later Europeanized by adding onions and replacing the game with chicken.

SUNNY BOY CEREAL—a breakfast fixture on Alberta tables since the 1920s. It is manufactured from organic grains by the Schroeder Milling Company, which also produces a line of quality bread and pancake mixes under the same label.

SUNROOT. *See* Jerusalem artichoke.

SUPPORNE—a thick, easily made porridge made from Indian meal, with a look and taste similar to oatmeal porridge. To pioneer families, supporne was breakfast and was prepared every morning without fail. All you do is sprinkle Indian meal on salted boiling water and stir for 20 minutes. Supporne is a real rib-sticker when eaten with milk and sugar, honey or maple syrup.

SWANS DOWN CAKE FLOUR—a favourite soft wheat cake flour of Canadian bakers since 1885, and now manufactured by Dover Mills of Cambridge, Ontario.

SWEET MARIE BAR—a fudge and peanut chocolate bar introduced by the Willard's Chocolate Company in 1931. Bought out by the George Weston Company in 1954, Willard's Sweet Marie bar is today manufactured by Cadbury, a new division of Kraft Foods.

SWEET POTATO CASSEROLE—a variation of pumpkin pudding and a Thanksgiving dessert of both pioneer and modern-day families. Boiled and mashed sweet potatoes are mixed with butter, eggs, cream, maple syrup, molasses or brown sugar, topped with a mixture of nuts, coconut, brown sugar, molasses or maple syrup, and baked.

SWEET VIBURNUM. *See* nannyberries.

SWITCHEL. *See* stenchel.

T

TABAC DES BOIS (also called powdered mushrooms)—a Quebec specialty, this mushroom powder can be wild or cultivated and is a favourite of upscale chefs.

TARTE AU SUCRE. *See* maple syrup pie.

TEABERRY. *See* wintergreen.

THORNLOE CHEESE—a northern Ontario cheese maker specializing in Cheddar and goat cheese and a consistent winner at the Royal Winter Fair. Their superlative Temis brand cheeses are available at Ontario and some Quebec retail outlets and online. Watch for their goat's milk blue cheese—it is a taste sensation.

THOUSAND ISLAND DRESSING—a salad dressing mix of mayonnaise, ketchup, Tabasco sauce and chopped pickle invented in the Thousand Islands area of Ontario and New York State.

TRIVIA

Thousand Island Dressing

Rumour has it that around 1900, when May Irwin, a New York stage actress, was visiting New York hotel owner George Bolt on Hart Island, his "one in a thousand islands," she received the recipe from Sophia Lalonde, the wife of her fishing guide, who got the recipe from her Quebecois mother. Irwin gave the recipe to Bolt, who gave it to the head chef of his Waldorf Astoria Hotel, who gave it to an appreciative public.

THREE SISTERS SOUP—a First Nations soup that uses the "three sisters" planting of corn, beans and squash.

> RECIPE
>
> *Three Sisters Soup, Modern Version*
>
> *Sauté ½ cup chopped onions and 1 tsp minced garlic in 3 Tbsp olive oil. Add 1 can each, with liquids, of corn, kidney beans and squash (or pumpkin), and water for desired consistency. Heat, season and serve with a dusting of black pepper.*

THRILLS CHEWING GUM—a Canadian original with rose water flavouring that most people equate to soap.

TIMPSULA. See *pomme-de-prairie*.

TOPINAMBOUR. *See* Jerusalem artichoke.

TOPINAMBOUR BEIGNETS. *See* Jerusalem artichoke fritters.

TORONTO MARMALADE (also called Toronto jam)— a homemade condiment of boiled grated tomatoes, lemons and sugar. Popular during both world wars owing to scarcity of tree fruits, the culinary endeavour produced an acceptable jam substitute.

TORONTO PIE—a hot milk sponge cake, split in half and filled with strawberry or raspberry jam and popular in Toronto during the latter half of the 19th century.

> RECIPE
>
> *Toronto Pie*
>
> *Mix 1 cup sugar, 3 eggs, 1½ cups flour, 1 tsp baking powder and flavour to taste. Bake as for jelly cake, then layer and spread jam between layers.*

TOURTIERE—iconic French Canadian pork pie with as many variations as there are towns in *la belle province*. One of the best—a layered meat and potatoes rib sticker—evolved in the Saguenay-Lac-St-Jean region. While tourtiere has many variations, it is usually a combination of ground or cubed pork or beef, onions, salt, pepper and spices enclosed within a flaky crust. You can find many tourtiere recipes online, and almost all are superior to the frozen tourtiere sold in supermarkets.

TRIVIA

Tourtiere

- Tourtiere likely arrived in the Lac-St-Jean area as a variation of sea pie, a layered meat and pastry provision for officers of English sailing ships that became entrenched in Atlantic coastal cuisine and was—and is still—called *cipaille*.

- *Tourte* is the French word for pigeon, once a main ingredient in tourtiere. It is also the name of the pottery vessel used to bake the original pie *avec tourtes*.

TOUTON—a Newfoundland treat of fried yeast-risen bread dough served hot and drenched with molasses or maple syrup.

TRIPE DE ROCHE. See famine foods. *See also* rock tripe.

TRITICALE—a Canadian Department of Agriculture cross-breed of wheat and rye, having the flavour of both. Developed for Third World countries with marginal agricultural land, the grain has found popularity at home in the form of nutritious breakfast flakes.

T

TROUT IN CORNHUSKS—a simple First Nations method of cooking trout adopted by settlers in Upper Canada (now Ontario). After larding and seasoning the fish, wrap it in stripped cornhusks and tie at both ends. Cover with campfire coals and cook for 15 minutes.

TURKEY *AU VIN*—a one-pot turkey masterpiece that in Canada's formative years would have featured wild turkey as the star attraction. Combined with onions, celery, carrots, mushrooms and a couple of cups of good red wine, this dish will tantalize diners even with a small commercial bird in the pot.

TURNIP CASSEROLE—ubiquitous in pioneer cuisine and easy to make. While not indigenous to Canada, as they arrived from France in 1541, turnips carried west by settlers and intended as cattle food were soon a prominent menu item. By the latter part of the 19th century, turnips had become a staple on Canadian dinner tables.

RECIPE

Turnip Casserole

Boil and mash 2 turnips. Add 1 cup applesauce, 2 Tbsp brown sugar, 1½ tsp salt, 6 Tbsp butter, 2 eggs and ¼ tsp pepper, and top with butter-sautéed breadcrumbs. Bake at 350° F for ½ hour or until top is brown and crispy.

T

U

UDDER GUYS ICE CREAM—a Vancouver Island delight made from the finest ingredients by Judy Piggot, the hardest-working gal to ever buck the dairy conglomerates.

UMI. *See* sea urchin roe.

V

VEAL—the tender meat of male dairy calves. To give milk, dairy cows must calve, and half of newborn calves are males and superfluous to the industry because insemination of milk cows is accomplished by artificial means. Female calves, or heifers, are generally kept as replacements for aging cows, while male, or bull, calves are sold off to veal producers.

RECIPE

Venison Pot Roast

Rub a 3–4 kg haunch of venison with vinegar, red pepper and salt, and lard with strips of salt pork (or bacon) rolled in seasoned bread crumbs. Prepare a marinade of red currant jelly, ½ cup dry red wine and 1 tsp each juniper berries, thyme, peppercorns, garlic, salt and molasses (or brown sugar). Allow venison to marinate a few hours. Brown haunch on all sides in a hot Dutch oven, pour on marinade, cover and roast at 350° F for 12 minutes per pound. Remove cover for the last 15 minutes. Serve with sauce.

For the sauce, reduce a mixture of venison scraps, 3 pints water, a few cloves, some mace, nutmeg, salt and a shake or two of cayenne pepper. Skim fat and strain; add 1 cup red currant jelly, 1 cup dry red wine and ¼ lb butter, divided into bits and rolled in flour.

V

VENISON LOIN WITH WINE SAUCE—the best cut of venison roasted and served in the manner of the earliest French dinner club, the Order of Good Cheer.

RECIPE

Venison Loin with Wine Sauce

Slice loin in pieces and mix up a marinade of olive oil, sliced carrots, celery, onions, garlic, thyme and bay leaves. Marinate in the refrigerator for 24 hours. Sprinkle with salt and pepper, and sear loin all sides. Roast in a preheated 400° F oven for 7–10 minutes or until cooked medium rare. Slice against the grain and serve with sauce.

To make sauce, reduce 3 cups beef stock to half and set aside. Cook ¼ cup minced shallots, 1 minced garlic clove and 1 thyme sprig until soft. Add 2 large, coarsely chopped tomatoes and cook for 5 minutes. Add 1 cup red wine, 3 Tbsp sherry wine vinegar and ¼ cup port wine, and boil until reduced by half. Add reserved stock, 2 Tbsp red currant jelly and simmer for 1 hour, skimming when necessary.

VENISON POT ROAST—a classic Sunday night pioneer dinner as delicious today as it was in earlier times.

VICTOR ET BERTHOLD CHEESE—a semi-soft, award-winning, raw Ayrshire cow's milk cheese made at the Fromagerie du Champ a la Meule, in Notre Dame de Lourdes, Quebec.

VIN DE MIEL. *See* Hydromel.

VINEGAR PIE—a prairie adaptation of lemon pie, made before the railway brought in fresh lemons. Prepared as regular lemon pie, but with lemon essence and vinegar, to raise acidity and tartness.

VOYAGEUR STEW—originally a game stew with salt bacon, pemmican, wild rice and dried peas, the recipe now includes beef broth, various vegetables and herbs.

V

W

WACKY CAKE (also called lazy cake, crazy cake, blue Monday cake)—a mix-in-the-pan chocolate cake popular during the 1950s and promoted by cooking maven Kate Aitken as the first cake young girls should learn to make.

WAFFLES—Canadians have carried on a long-time love affair with waffles. In the early days, stovetops were the cooking vehicle, and Indian corn batter was poured into an iron mould constructed by a local blacksmith. Nowadays, batter can be any grain and waffles are cooked in electric waffle makers, but the maple syrup topping has stayed the same, and that is what a waffle is all about.

WALLEYE (*Sander vitreus* [formerly *Stizostedion vitreum*]; also called pickerel, dore)—an important food source for First Nations, and familiar to early pioneer settlers because the fish also ranges in lakes and rivers in Europe. Walleye abound in the Great Lakes, and in northern waters they are the dominant species. Walleye flesh is white and flaky and is considered by many people to be the world's tastiest freshwater fish. They are caught commercially in many areas of Canada. Walleye are also an important game fish and account for millions in tourist revenues, especially to Saskatchewan, where the species is the provincial fish.

WALLEYE IN BEER BATTER—a favourite shore lunch recipe of fishermen.

WALLEYE

In years past, a variety of blue walleye found in the Great Lakes watershed was so popular that it became fished out by the late 1950s. During that time, my father had a standing order with the Erie Beach Motel in Port Dover for blue pickerel. Whenever commercial fishermen caught one in their nets, the Erie Beach would call my dad, and he would drop everything and race the seven miles to Port Dover to feast on the rarity. His last rush to the blue occurred in spring 1958; after that, the Erie Beach never called again.

RECIPE

Walleye in Beer Batter

Beat 3 eggs until frothy, add ½ can beer and 1 tsp salt. In another bowl, combine 1 cup each cornmeal and flour with 1 tsp salt. Dip skinless walleye fillets into liquid batter, roll in dry mix and fry in butter until golden and the fish flakes with a fork.

WAR CAKE—a recipe popular in World War I when some baking ingredients were missing from store shelves. War cake bakers used flour, corn syrup, water, salt, cloves and nutmeg to produce a heavy, fruitcake-type cake with good keeping qualities.

WATER AVENS. *See* Indian chocolate.

WATER OATS. *See* wild rice.

WATERCRESS SOUP—a fresh-tasting cress and potato soup favoured by pioneer settlers and modern-day upscale chefs.

259

> **RECIPE**
>
> *Watercress Soup*
>
> *Sauté 2 chopped onions in 2 Tbsp butter. Add 2 bunches watercress and 2 peeled and diced potatoes, and cook, stirring, for 5 minutes. Add 2 cups chicken broth and lower heat. Simmer for 15 minutes. Run mixture through sieve, food mill or blender, return to pan and add 2 cups milk, and salt and pepper. Serve hot with a dab of butter.*

WEESUKAPUKA. *See* Labrador tea.

WESTERN SANDWICH—a waste-not, want-not sandwich invention of early prairie settlers. In the heat of summer, fresh eggs without refrigeration spoiled quickly, and to avoid having to discard them, pioneer cooks would disguise the off flavour by mixing them with onions, salt pork, peppers, etc.

WHEAT BERRIES—kernels of wheat straight from the farmer's field. Used in salads, wheat berries are first softened by long boiling (1½ hours), then cooled, seasoned and added to greens or various culinary preparations, or frozen for later use.

WHEAT BREAD—any bread made from any variety of the hybridized seeds of the grass plant *Triticum* spp. *See also* bread.

WHEAT BREAD

Wheat (and wheat bread) has as much history in Canada as its people: both arrived around the same time. The first wheat seeds went into the ground at Port Royal in spring 1606, and the first loaves of Canadian wheat bread were baked that fall. Since then, both our people and those seeds have evolved, the former into a great nation, the latter into the best bread-making wheat on the planet.

WHISKY. *See* applejack, cherry whisky, rye whisky, single malt whisky, Yukon Jack whisky.

WHITE HATTER STEW—a baked, pastry-topped beef stew and the official grub of the Calgary Stampede. One-pot meals were a mainstay of chuckwagon cooks, and that tradition continues at the Stampede. White hatter stew is usually served up in individually baked containers to the sea of white-hatted visitors.

WHITE WALNUT SOUP. *See* butternut soup.

WHITEFISH—grilled, baked, fried: it matters not, as this freshwater delight is sure to please. Whitefish are popular in Canada and account for a third of the value of the inland fishery.

WHOOPEE PIE—a traditional Mennonite iced cookie still available at farmers' markets where Mennonites sell their farm and kitchen products.

WHORE'S EGGS. *See* cosy eggs.

WILD ASPARAGUS. *See* milkweed.

WILD BERRY JUMBLE PIE—raspberries, saskatoons, blackberries, cranberries, strawberries, nagoonberries, mossberries, gooseberries, blueberries, squashberries, salalberries, elderberries, salmonberries, partridgeberries, mooseberries, jostaberries and huckleberries. Dewberries, lingonberries, currants red and black, nannyberries, bakeapples, teaberries and buffaloberries. And dozens more, along with many suitable only as famine food. When berries are picked as found, several kinds will go into the pail, and who wants to sort berries? Poured onto the pie crust in one delicious jumble, an epicurean masterpiece will often emerge from the oven. It's not strictly Canadian, since jumble pie has been around for ages, but the berries are distinctly so and provide us rightful claim to this luscious wild berry pie.

WILD BERRIES

Wild berries added zest to pemmican and provided early settlers a welcome addition to corn mush and rabbit stew. Dried berries made a passable substitute for raisins in dessert recipes, while fresh berries made marvellous jams and jellies with or without added sweeteners.

Wild berry bushes also provided Canadian settlers with a virtual pharmacy for common ailments, as their bark, berries and leaves contain all manner of medicinal properties. Highbush cranberry tea cured swollen glands and dampered the effects of mumps. A wine fermented from sweet, ripe hawberries could be cheerfully imbibed to cure pains, ague and bladder problems. Pin cherries cured scurvy and the common cold. Chokecherries cured diarrhea, while a decoction of black cherry root would prevent diarrhea. The dug up roots of blueberry plants infused in water produced a palatable tea that reputedly cured both cholera and hiccups. And lowbush cranberries cured dysentery, a common ailment among early settlers. Settlers near Ontario's Lake Erie region had a special treat in the bay, or wax myrtle; its wax-covered berries not only cured scrofula but, mixed with beeswax, also produced scented candles, a fortuitous discovery to occupants of tiny cabins, even in modern times.

TRIVIA

Wild Berries

Most of Canada's wild and cultivated berries are related members of the Rose family, while the cranberry, huckleberry and blueberry are members of the Heath family.

W

WILD CELERY. *See* Indian celery.

WILD CITRON. *See* mayapple.

WILD COTTON. *See* milkweed.

WILD GINGER (*Asarum canadense*; also called Canada snake-root, Indian ginger)—from the root is extracted a flavouring agent with a remarkable ginger flavour. Employed by native peoples and early settlers as a cookery seasoning and wine/beer additive, peeled wild ginger root was an important trade item for many years.

WILD GINGER ALERT

Wild ginger root was recently found to contain aristolochic acid, a known carcinogen, and efforts have been made by government agencies to deter foraging of this once-popular seasoning.

WILD JALAP. *See* mayapple.

WILD LEEK (*Allium tricoccum*; also called ramp, rampion)— a member of the Onion family and much used by native peoples and settlers to flavour game and stews. Although identical in flavour, wild leeks growing in western Canada sport narrow leaves, while the eastern variant has broader leaves.

TRIVIA

Wild Leek

Not just a good substitute for garlic, the wild leek is also purported to provide almost mystical health benefits: it lowers blood sugar and corrects hypertension, speeds healing of wounds and cures both freckles and the common cold.

WILD LICORICE. *See* licorice root.

WILD MUSTARD. *See* charlock.

WILD RAISINS. *See* nannyberries.

WILD RICE (*Zizania palustris*, *Z. aquatica*; also called Canada rice, Indian rice, water oats)—while not true rice, wild rice is a close relative. Both are grasses from the same family, Oryzeae. Globally, four species exist: wild rice (*Z. aquatica*), northern wild rice (*Z. palustris*), Texas wild rice (*Z. texana*) and an Asian species, Manchurian wild rice (*Z. latifolia*). Never of any commercial or dietary importance, Texas wild rice has all but disappeared, while the Manchurian species, a one-time a staple food for the Chinese, became less so with the advent of easier-to-grow rice species, and it too has all but disappeared. Not so with the wild and northern species—both were mainstay foods of First Nations and Canadian and American settlers, and they have continued to grow in popularity, with the northern species being the most commonly harvested.

WILD RICE

The ricing, or harvesting, of wild rice is a technique perfected by First Nations and is called knocking. Old-style knocking entails driving a flat-bottomed canoe into a stand of wild rice, bending the stalks over the craft with one long stick and knocking that stick with another called the knocker. Done properly, knocked rice grains fall off the stalks and into the bottom of the canoe in neat piles. Done improperly, the stalks may break, negating a second or third ricing. Nowadays, most ricers use flat-bottomed airboats with a mechanized knocker and collecting tray, but the need for proper technique remains unchanged: a ricer must knock with the boat at the proper speed or risk damaging the plants. Wild rice is an annual plant, and knockers must take care to allow some grains to remain as seed for their next season's crop.

Once harvested, rice grains must be dried quickly to prevent mildew. Years ago, before the arrival of the Europeans, drying was accomplished by layering the grains on a large platform over several small fires. With the Europeans came large iron pots that enabled the parching, or slow roasting, of rice grains, a process still in use today. Slow roasting drives out moisture, destroys the germ—thus preventing germination—and hardens off the kernel. The hull loosens and falls away during "hulling," a process that used to involve tedious hours of treading on rice grains until they became separated from their hulls but is now accomplished by machines at local buying depots or tribal mills. Winnowing, or cleaning, the grains of chaff is also done by a depot or mill machine, but in the old days, it usually involved throwing the grains into the air, allowing the wind to remove chaff and bits of undesirable matter. In times past, wild rice grains packed into animal skin sacks or birchbark containers and buried in the ground below the frost line would keep for long periods. Nowadays, grains processed by depot machines come in paper sacks or boxes not designed to protect them for long periods, but that is never a problem because naturally harvested wild rice is much in demand.

In Canada, both Saskatchewan and Manitoba provide discriminating consumers and chefs worldwide with natural wild rice that is both tasty and nutritious. Wild rice is high in protein, low in fat, a good source of potassium and vitamins riboflavin, thiamin and niacin, and makes a wonderful side for any main dish, especially wild duck.

TRIVIA

Wild Rice

- Ricers have generational claim to productive areas and, while not necessary in modern times, ricer families used to bind rice stalks into bundles as a way of marking territory, with each family using a unique form of binding, such as different strips of bark or ways of tying the bundles.

- Ricing is not without its hazards, as the grains are sharp enough to pierce skin, and some grains harbour rice worms that can inflict nasty bites. Needless to say, ricers go well protected even in sweltering heat. In Manitoba and Saskatchewan, First Nations are the major harvesters, and their ricing garb has remained little changed for better than 200 years: lots of protection and plenty of spruce gum to remove barbs from the eyes.

WILD SPINACH. *See* lamb's quarters.

WILD TURNIP. See *pomme-de-prairie*.

WILLY KRAUCH'S SMOKED FISH—salmon, mackerel and eel, and according to Craig Claiborne, late food writer of the *New York Times*, nobody smokes them better than Willy Krauch does. Willy passed away a few years ago, but his three kids are still keeping Tangier, PEI, the subject of food columnists around the globe.

WINDSOR BEAN. *See* horse bean.

WINNIPEG GOLDEYE (*Hiodon alosoides*)—a small, freshwater fish with a deep body and large, yellow eyes. Endemic to rivers and lakes from Ontario to BC, goldeyes are caught commercially in Manitoba and Saskatchewan and processed in Winnipeg.

There, gutted fish are brined, dyed an orange colour, smoked over oak fires, boxed and shipped worldwide.

> ## RECIPE
>
> *Winnipeg Goldeye*
>
> *Bake fish at 450° F for 12–15 minutes, remove the skin and backbone, and serve on toast.*

WINNIPEG GOLDEYE AND CRAB CAKES—an Alberta discovery that raises crab cakes to a culinary level that surpasses the American effort by miles—sorry, by kilometres.

> ## RECIPE
>
> *Winnipeg Goldeye and Crab Cakes*
>
>
>
> *Sauté 1 diced onion, 1 diced bell pepper and 1 diced stalk of celery in butter until soft. Add 2 tsp chopped fresh tarragon, zest of 1 lemon and 1 tsp Worcestershire sauce, and set aside to cool. In a large bowl, mix 1 lb each cleaned crab meat and Winnipeg goldeye with the diced onion mixture, 2 tsp Dijon mustard, salt and pepper to taste, 2 beaten eggs and 3 cups breadcrumbs, or enough to hold cakes together. Form mix into cakes. Place seasoned flour on one plate and seasoned breadcrumbs on another plate. Make an egg wash in a shallow bowl. Dredge crab cakes in seasoned flour, then dip into egg wash, and then roll in seasoned breadcrumbs. Pan fry in butter until golden brown, then transfer to a preheated 375° F oven and bake for 8–10 minutes or until done. Just the best.*

W

WINTERGREEN (*Gaultheria procumbens*; also called boxberry, checkerberry, teaberry, partridgeberry)—a low-growing, cross-Canada evergreen groundcover with bright red berries that persist well into winter and provide pickers a waxy, sweet chew. During the late 19th and early 20th centuries, both the leaves and the berries were commercially foraged to make flavouring for jelly, candy, toothpaste and gum. Wintergreen flavouring is still popular, but it is now made artificially.

TRIVIA

Wintergreen

Got a toothache? A wintergreen leaf placed on the affected tooth will alleviate the pain like magic. Wintergreen also supposedly increases blood circulation to the gums, an attribute that probably gave rise to the toothpaste flavouring.

WINTERGREEN CANDY—a Turkish delight–style candy perfected by herbalist and 1960s TV personality Euell Gibbons.

WINTERGREEN TEA—a hot water decoction of the fermented leaves of the wintergreen plant, and a much-used settlers' tonic for whatever ailed them. The essential oil in wintergreen, oil of wintergreen, is 99 percent methyl salicylate, which is in the same chemical family as aspirin.

WINTERGREEN WINE—a favourite of pioneer women for the way it livened up functions such as quilting and canning bees, and old-time herbalists recommended wintergreen wine be given to invalids as a pick-me-up.

WISHAKAPUKA. *See* Labrador tea.

X Y Z

XIPHIAS (Latin for swordfish, and as close as I could get to a Canadian food word beginning with the letter X)—swordfish (*Xiphias gladius*) are large billfish with a streamlined body that helps propel them through the water at speeds in excess of 100 kilometres per hour when chasing prey. They are a migratory fish and spend summers in Nova Scotia's warm Gulf Stream waters, and their annual presence supports a harpoon fishery with a long history. Swordfish are caught individually and on the surface by a harpoon launched by hand from a chase boat. They are also caught in great numbers by commercial long liners, but Maritimers care little for long dead on a hook and insist their swordfish steaks come from harpooned fish, as they have for centuries. The next time you want swordfish for the barbecue, ask your fishmonger if his steaks are harpooned or caught by long line. If the latter, tell him to smarten up and get the good stuff.

YORKSHIRE PUDDING WITH WILD RICE—east met west in a Canada West settler's kitchen, and the dish remained a favourite until hearth cooking saw replacement by kitchen stoves and meat juices no longer dripped off roasts, but pooled in pots. Easy to make: simply include precooked wild rice in any standard Yorkshire pudding recipe, pour into pudding pans or a casserole dish and bake at 450° F until tall, brown and scrumptious looking.

X
Y
Z

YUKON GOLD POTATO—a Canadian original developed by botanist Gary Johnston at the University of Guelph during the early 1960s and now grown worldwide.

YUKON GOLD POTATO FRENCH FRIES—in the hierarchy of diabolical, "wish we hadn't thought of that" modern-day inventions, frozen French fries are right up there with gas-powered leaf blowers, aluminum cans and plastic bottles—shameful inventions, icons of laziness. The frozen French fry is the only one we can do anything about, because a better product can be made in the home kitchen.

RECIPE

Yukon Gold Fries

Trim 6 large Yukon Gold potatoes into cubes. Cut the spuds into strips and place into a plastic bag with 3–4 Tbsp olive oil (maybe some onion and garlic too) and shake. Lay strips on a well-greased pan, season and bake at 375° F for 15 minutes, then flip and bake another 15 minutes, or until crisp. They're way better than frozen, and a whole lot healthier.

YUKON JACK WHISKY—named after celebrated Yukon pioneer Captain Jack McQuesten, this 100 proof, honey-based whisky liqueur is the celebrated "puts hair on your chest" drink of our Yukon and Northwest Territories.

ZUCCHINI—a variety of summer squash developed in Italy from North American origins. Now grown in gardens across Canada for its edible flowers and fruit, it is best picked small before it has a chance to go out of control and you end up abandoning it on neighbours' doorsteps in the middle of the night. *See also* squash.

X
Y
Z

Sources

Barss, Beulah M. *The Pioneer Cook*. Calgary: 1931; Calgary: Detselig Enterprises Ltd., 1980.

Berton, Pierre and Janet. *Canadian Food Guide*. Toronto: McClelland and Stewart, 1966.

Breckenridge, Muriel. *The Old Ontario Cook Book*. Toronto: McGraw-Hill Ryerson Limited, 1976.

Casselman, Bill. *Canadian Food Words*. Toronto: McArthur & Company, 1998.

———. *Canadian Words and Sayings*. Toronto: McArthur & Company, 2006.

Duncan, Dorothy. *Canadians at Table*. Toronto: Dundurn Press, 2006.

Ellis, Eleanor A. *Northern Cookbook*. Edmonton: Hurtig Publishers, 1967.

Erichsen-Brown, Charlotte. *Medicinal and Other Uses of North American Plants*. New York: Dover Publications, 1979.

Ferguson, Carol and Margaret Fraser. *A Century of Canadian Home Cooking*. Toronto: Prentice Hall Canada Inc., 1992.

Fritsch, Klaus with Mary Goodbody. *Morton's Steak Bible*. New York: Clarkson Potter, 2006.

Gibbons, Euell. *Stalking the Healthful Herb*. New York: David McKay Company, 1966.

Kurlansky, Mark. *Cod*. Toronto: Alfred A. Knopf, 1997.

Lafrance, Marc and Yvon Desloges. *A Taste of History*. Montreal: Les Editions de la Cheneliere and Canadian Park Services, 1989.

Laura Secord Candy Shops. *Laura Secord Canadian Cook Book*. Toronto: McClelland and Stewart, 1984.

Murray, Rose. *A Taste of Canada*. Vancouver: Whitecap Books, 2008.

Nearing, Helen and Scott. *The Maple Sugar Book*. New York: Schoken Books, 1950.

Ogle, Jennifer. *Canadian Cookbook*. Edmonton: Lone Pine Publishing, 2006.

Pringle, Laurence. *Wild Foods*. New York: Four Winds Press, 1978.

Purity Flour Canadian Cook Book. Toronto: Coles Publishing Company Limited, 1975.

Rolland, Jacques L. *The Cook's Essential Kitchen Dictionary*. Toronto: Robert Rose Inc., 2004.

Staebler, Edna. *Food That Really Schmecks*. Toronto: The Ryerson Press, 1968.

Stewart, Anita. *Our Mothers' Kitchen*. Toronto: Random House, 1991.

———. *The Flavours of Canada*. Vancouver: Raincoast Books, 2000.

Traill, Catharine Parr. *The Backwoods of Canada*. London, England: Charles Knight,1836; Toronto: Penguin Canada, 2006.

———. *The Canadian Settlers Guide*. Toronto: Toronto Times, 1857; Toronto: McClelland and Stewart, 1996.

The Cook Not Mad. Kingston: James Macfarlane, 1831; Toronto: The Cherry Tree Press, 1973.

Upton, L.F.S. *Micmacs and Colonists*. Vancouver: University of BC Press, 1979.

ONLINE
Statistics Canada.